Woman and the Sea

BOOKS BY MICHÆL MOTT

POETRY

The Cost of Living (1957)
The Tales of Idiots and New Exile (1962)
A Book of Pictures (1962)
Absence of Unicorns, Presence of Lions (1976)
Counting the Grasses (1980)
Corday (1986; reprinted 1995)
Piero di Cosimo: The World of Infinite Possibility (1990)
Taino (1992)

NOVELS

The Notebooks of Susan Berry (1963)
Helmet and Wasps (1966)
Master Entrick, juvenile (1966)
The Blind Cross, juvenile (1969)

BIOGRAPHY

The Seven Mountains of Thomas Merton (1984)

Woman and the Sea

Selected poems by Michael Mott

Edited by
Walton Beacham

Introduction by
George Garrett

ANHINGA PRESS, 1998
TALLAHASSEE, FLORIDA

Library of Congress Card Catalog Number: 96-083909
ISBN: 0-938078-44-5

Printed in the United States of America

Cover art by Margaret Mott
Cover Design by Lynne Knight
Book design and production by Geoffrey Brock and Lynne Knight

*This publication is sponsored in part by a grant from the
Florida Department of State, Division of Cultural Affairs,
and the Florida Arts Council.*

Anhinga Press is a nonprofit corporation dedicated wholly
to the publication and appreciation of fine poetry.

ANHINGA PRESS
P.O. Box 10595
Tallahassee, FL 32302
www.anhinga.org

Contents

V — AMERICA, THE HAUNTED LAND
Part One: The Civil War

IX — ANARCHY AND FAITH

X — CIRCE AND HER LOVERS (LOVE AND WAR)

Acknowledgements

Grateful acknowledgment is made to the publishers and editors who have kindly allowed work to be reprinted in this book.

Poems were taken from the following collections:

The Cost of Living (TCOL), *Adam International Review*, Adam Books, U.K., 1957.
A Book of Pictures (BP), Outposts Publications, U.K., 1962.
Absence of Unicorns, Presence of Lions (UNICORNS), Little, Brown, Boston, Feb. 1976.
Counting the Grasses (CG), Anhinga Press, Nov. 1980.

Other collections and chapbooks —*The Tales of Idiots* and *New Exile* (1962); *Corday* (1986, reprinted 1995); *Piero di Cosimo: The World of Infinite Possibility* (1990); and *Taino* (1992) — are each made up of a single poem or a group of poems on a unified theme and it seemed impossible to represent any of them here. *Corday* is in print and available from Black Buzzard Press, 1007 Ficklen Road, Fredericksburg, VA 22405.

Amour Propre: Clarence may be the earliest poem here, and the first to be printed and reprinted. I remember writing it at Oxford in the Spring of 1951. The most recent is Manqué, which was written Jan. 19, 1995. For this reason, and because so many poems here have appeared only in reviews and not in collections, it was thought that it might be interesting to combine acknowledgments with a brief note on the date of composition (where this can be established) and the history of publication (using the code given above for collections.)

I

Red Leaves: written Oct. 30, 1981; revised 1993; first published *Visions*, No. 45, Fall 1994.

Harpsichord in the Rain: written Sept. 9, 1976; first published *The Hampden-Sydney Poetry Review*, Winter 1976-77; *Poets in the South, 1977-78*; CG, 1980; *The Hampden-Sydney Poetry Review Anthology, 1975-1990*, 1990.

Woman and the Sea: written Summer 1972; first published UNICORNS, 1976; *Poets in the South, 1977-78*.

Wisteria: written Fall 1976; first published *The Hampden-Sydney Poetry Review*, Winter 1976-77; *The Hampden-Sydney Poetry Review Anthology, 1975-1990*, 1990.

Juniper: written 1976; first published *Poetry*, Vol. CXXIX, No. 6, March 1977; *Poets in the South, 1977-78*; CG, 1980.

Etruscan Mirrors: written about 1958; first published BP, 1962; *Poets in the South, 1977-78*.

Poem: written about 1956; first published TCOL, 1957.

In Memory of William Stafford 1914–1993: written Oct. 30, 1993; first published *The Sewanee Review*, Vol. CII, No. 3, Summer 1994.

The Sheep: written Feb. 1972; first published *The Mississippi Review*, Vol. IV, No. 1, 1977.

Tarn: written May 1981; first published *The Sewanee Review*, Vol. XCI, No. 2, Spring 1983; *The Kenyon Poets Anthology*, Fall 1989.

The Defeat of Names: written 1963-64; first published *The Fiddlehead* (Canada), No. 71, Spring 1967; *The Borestone Mountain Poetry Awards, Best Poems of 1967.*

II

The Letters: almost all were written in the fall of 1974. A few, like Myths XIII, were written earlier (April 13, 1971). The group was first published in UNICORNS, 1976. Myths VIII and Myths XXIII were republished in *Poets in the South, 1977-78.*

III

Proteus: written 1976; first published *Canto*, Vol. II, No. 2, Summer 1978; CG, 1980.

Light-Year: written Fall 1972-Spring 1973; first published *Poetry*, Vol. CXXV, No. 3, Dec. 1974; UNICORNS, 1976. Winter Solstice appeared separately in *The Callanwolde Poets*, 1976 and in *Poets in the South, 1977-78.*

Shadows of Leaves You Cross: written in 1962; first published *The Fiddlehead* (Canada), No. 71, Spring 1967.

"Birdless": written Mar. 1981; first published *Tar River Poetry Review*, Vol. XXV, No. 2, Spring 1967.

Arachne's Island: written 1967; first published *Arion: A Journal of the Humanities and the Classics*, Vol, VII, No. 1, Spring 1968.

Islanders, Inlanders: written Fall 1969; first published *Poetry*, Vol. CXVI, April 1970; *Poetry Anthology 1912-1977*, 1978; CG, 1980.

From A Personal Alphabet: written Spring 1971. *Poetry* published: "A", "B", "C", "E", "M", "S", "W", Vol. CXX, No. 1, April 1972. "Z" was first published in *The Dekalb Literary Arts Journal*, No. 18, July 1972. *Poem* published "K", "P", "Q", "R", in No. 18, July 1973. *The Andover Review* published "B" and "C" in Vol. I, Summer 1974.

First Primer: written 1954; first published TCOL, 1957.

Modigliani: written 1953; first published *Adam International Review*, No. 256, 1956; TCOL, 1957.

The Coat: written 1960; revised 1996; early version published *Adam International Review*, No. 300, 1965.

The Dice: written Feb. 1973; first published *Poetry*, Vol. CXXIII, No. 1, Oct. 1973; UNICORNS, 1976.

Jonah: written 1959; first published *The Georgia Review*, Vol. XXVIII, No. 2, Summer 1974.

Familiars: written Summer 1972; first published *Encounter* (U.K.), Dec. 1972.

The Whale's Lament for the Lost Whalers: written 1977; first published *The Hampden-Sydney Poetry Review*, Summer 1978.

Lessons: written May 1973; first published *The Andover Review*, Vol. 1, No. 2, Fall 1974.

Urban Streams: written Fall 1969; first published *The Southern Review*, Vol. 7, No. 2, April 1971.

Homage to St. Neot and His Church: written Oct. 27, 1970; first published *Encounter* (U.K.), Oct. 1971; CG 1980.

Pastoral: written 1966; revised 1969; first published *Poetry*, Vol. CXVI, No. 1, April 1970; *UNICORNS*, 1976.

Past Newfoundland: written 1966; revised 1969; first published *Prairie Schooner*, Vol. XLVI, No. 3, Fall 1972. Reprinted by permission of the University of Nebraska Press. Copyright 1972, University of Nebraska Press.

Autumn, Odysseus: written 1962; revised 1981; revised 1989; first published *Tar River Poetry Review*, Vol. XXXIII, No. 1, Fall 1993; also printed in the program when Aequalis have performed "A Window Always Open On The Sea," which was commissioned from the composer Marilyn Shrude in 1990. The piece for cello, piano and percussion has been widely performed. Marilyn Shrude uses lines from the poem for each section of the work.

IV

Sir John By Starlight: written 1959; first published *The Kenyon Review*, Vol. 26, No. 2, Spring 1964; *Borestone Mountain Poetry Awards, Best Poems of 1964*; *UNICORNS*, 1976; *Poets in the South, 1977-78*; *The Kenyon Poets Anthology*, Fall 1989.

Hamlet: written 1989; first published *The Sewanee Review*, Vol. CI, No. 4, Fall 1993.

April 23rd: written April 1976; first published *International Poetry Review*, Vol. V, No. 1, Spring 1979.

The Case: written 1975; first published *International Poetry Review*, Vol. V, No. 1, Spring 1979.

Madrigal with an Echo: written Sept. 1976; first published *New Virginia Review*, Vol. I, 1978-79.

Lines For Queen Gertrude: written 1971; first published *Tar River Poetry Review*, Vol. XXIX, No. 1, Fall 1989.

Horatio's Soliloquy: written 1964; first published *The Sewanee Review*, Vol. XCV, No. 4, Fall 1987.

King Lear Poem: written Nov. 1969; first published *The Sewanee Review*, Vol. XCV, No. 4, Fall 1987 (where it was published under the editor's title, "Ripeness Is All").

Letter to Thomas Hariot: written April 21, 1970; revised 1974; revised 1986; first published *The Sewanee Review*, Vol. XCVII, No. 3, Summer 1989.

Letter to Goethe: written Oct. 27, 1970; first published *Encounter* (U.K.), April 1971.

For Wise Men: written 1963; first published *The Kenyon Review*, Vol. 26, No. 2, Spring 1964.

Dido: written 1958; first published *BP*, 1962.

Medea at Colonus: written 1979; first published *The William and Mary Review*, Vol. XVII, No. 2, Spring 1979.

Great and Small: written 1958; first published *BP*, 1962.

Motto: written Aug. 1988; first published *Tar River Poetry Review*, Vol. XXIX, No. 1, Fall 1989.

Fish Course: written Sept. 1975; first published *The Devil's Millhopper*, Spring 1980.

Musée Imaginaire: written Oct. 1971; first published *International Poetry Review*, Vol. IV, No. 2, Summer 1978.

Letter to Mistress Eleanor Gwyn: written 1970; revised 1990; first published *The Sewanee Review*, Vol. XCVIII, No. 4, Fall 1990.

Potiphar's Wife: written Nov. 1975; first published *Maxy's Journal*, No. 1, 1978.

Homage to Constantine Cavafy: written 1970; first published *Scarecrow Poetry: The Muse in Post-Middle Age Anthology*, Ashland Poetry Press, 1994.

Byron at Missolonghi: written in the winter of 1975; revised 1992; first published *The Sewanee Review*, Vol. CI, No. 3, Fall 1993.

Stendhal's Miss Appleby: written April 1982; revised 1987; first published *Tar River Poetry Review*, Vol. XXVI, No. 2, Spring 1988.

Rimbaud at Marseilles: written 1958; first published *BP*, 1962.

The Fires of the Fathers: written 1974; revised 1977; first published *CG*, 1980.

Report from Rheims: written 1988; revised Aug. 9-10, 1994; first published *Image: A Journal of the Arts and Religion*, No. 11, Fall 1995.

Manqué: written Jan. 19, 1995; first published *The American Scholar*, Volume 65, No. 4, Autumn 1996.

V
PART ONE

Kennesaw Mountain: written July 1969; first published *The Southern Review*, Vol. VII, No. 2, April 1971; *UNICORNS*, 1976.

Above Dalton: written March 30, 1974; first published *Southern Poetry Review*, Summer 1975; *UNICORNS*, 1976; *Poets in the South, 1977-78*.

Chickamauga: written July 1973; first published *UNICORNS*, 1976.

Shiloh: written summer 1972; early version published in *The Dekalb Literary Arts Journal*, No. 4, 1974; corrected version *Richmond Center for the Arts*, 1976; *UNICORNS*, 1976; *Poets in the South, 1977-78*.

Sourwood Mountain Song: written Mar. 31, 1974; first published *The Mississippi Review*, Vol. IV, No. 1, Summer 1975; *UNICORNS*, 1976; *Poets in the South, 1977-78.*

Gaines Mill: written July 1973; first published *UNICORNS*, 1976.

Sentry: written March 26, 1974; first published *Cold Mountain Review*, No. 2, Fall 1974, *UNICORNS*, 1976.

Mountain Laurel: written April 3, 1974; first published *Maxy's Journal*, No. 1, 1978.

Malvern Hill: written July 1973; first published UNICORNS, 1976.

Chimborazo: written July 1973; first published *Southern Poetry Review*, Vol. XX, No. 3, Fall 1980.

Peggy Lee Douglas at the Dulcimer: written 1974; first published *Cold Mountain Review*, No. 2, Fall 1974; UNICORNS, 1976.

Cold Harbor: written 1973; first published *New Orleans Review*, Vol. IV, No. 3, Summer 1973; *Poets in the South, 1977-78*; CG,1980.

Ropeburn: written March 31, 1974; first published *The Appalachian Journal*, Vol. III, No. 2, Winter 1976.

Mirabelle: written 1974; first published *The Georgia Review*, Vol. XXIX, No. 2, Summer 1975; UNICORNS, 1976.

Driving Through Butterflies in Kentucky: written Dec. 1980; first published *Adena*, Vol. VI, No. 1, Spring 1981.

Notes Toward a History of Kentucky: written Aug. 1981; first published *Kentucky Poetry Review*, Vol. XVIII, No. 1, Spring 1982.

Fort Blakely: written Feb. 1981; first published *William and Mary Review*, Vol. 19, No. 2, Spring 1982.

Driving Through the Wilderness, North Virginia, in a Blizzard to Rachmaninov: written Dec. 1985; first published in *Verse*, Vol. 3, No. 3, Fall 1986.

PART TWO

Unfinished America: written 1973; first published UNICORNS, 1976.

Far Floridas: written 1973; first published UNICORNS, 1976.

North West Passaging: written March 26, 1974; first published UNICORNS, 1976; *Poets in the South, 1977-78*.

Ibo: written 1973; first published *Cold Mountain Review*, No. 2, Fall 1974; *Outposts* (U.K.), No. 112, Spring 1977; CG, 1980.

Ohio Window: written Jan. 1967; first published *The Missouri Review*, Vol. IX, Nos. 3 & 4, Fall 1969; CG, 1980.

Las Milpas, New Mexico: written July 1967; first published *Prairie Schooner*, Vol. XLIV, No. 3, Fall 1969. Reprinted by permission of University of Nebraska. Copyright 1969 University of Nebraska Press. Copyright renewed 1997, University of Nebraska Press; CG, 1980.

Taos Pueblo: written July 1967; first published *The Colorado Quarterly*, Vol. XVI, No. 4, Spring 1968.

Not Seeing For Looking: written Sept. 1981; first published *The William and Mary Review*, Vol. 19, No. 2, Spring 1982.

Four River Songs: written March 1982; first published *The Kentucky Poetry Review,* Vol. 21, No. 1, Spring 1985.

Ohio, Winter Edge of Morning: written Jan. 1981; first published *Adena,* Vol. VI, No. 1, Spring 1981.

Geese on the Genesee: written March 23, 1981; first published *The Sewanee Review,* Vol. XCI, No. 2, Spring 1983.

Lament for Mary Macleod: written Oct. 5, 1977; first published *Off P'tree,* Fall 1977;   CG, 1980.

Our Third President: written 1973; first published *Southern Voices,* Vol. I, No. 1, Jan. 1974; UNICORNS, 1976.

Courbet in Georgia: written Sept. 1976; first published *A Local Muse,* No. 2, May 1977; CG, 1980.

Labor Day Weekend, North Georgia: written Sept. 9, 1976; first published *Cold Mountain Review,* No. 5, Fall 1977.

Bathsheba Come Morning: written Dec. 22, 1980; first published *Adena,* Vol. VI, No. 1, Spring 1981.

PART THREE

Cabin Between Creeks: written March 1983; first published *Tar River Poetry Review,* Vol. XXV, No. 2, Spring 1986.

Deer Mouse: written March 26-28, 1983, revised 1995; early version first published as "Deermice" in *The New Virginia Review,* Vol. VI, Nov. 1988.

The Pierce Poems: written Oct. 1978; first published in *Green River Review,* Vol. X, No. 3, Fall 1979; CG, 1980.

VI

The Well: written June 1972; first published *The Georgia Review,* Vol. XXVIII, No. 2, Summer 1974; *Poets in the South, 1977-78;* CG,1980.

Magnolia: written 1970; first published *The Mediterranean Review,* Vol. IV, No. 2, Winter 1971; *Poets in the South, 1977-78;* CG, 1980.

Osprey: written June 22, 1978; first published *Adena,*Vol. VI, No. 1, Spring 1981.

Cedar Waxwings Drunk on Berries: written 1975; first published *The New Virginia Review,* Vol. I, 1978-79; CG, 1980.

Catspaw: written 1977; first published *The Atlanta Gazette,* May 25, 1977; CG, 1980; *Poets in the South,* 1984.

Good Friday, 1978: written 1978; first published *Cairn,* Vol.15, Nos. 1 & 2, 1978-79; *Poets in the South, 1977-78;* CG, 1980. (*Poets in the South* appeared late.)

Sunday Morning: written Spring 1972; first published *Outposts* (U.K.), No. 106, Autumn 1975; CG, 1980.

Tree Struck By Lightning: written Sept. 22, 1992; first published *The Virginia Quarterly Review*, Vol. 70, No.3, Summer 1994.

In Praise of Our Days: written 1973; first published *Sundog*, Vol. II, Spring 1980; CG, 1980.

Meadow Grass: written June 22, 1978; first published *Poetry*, Vol. CXXIV, No. 1, April 1979; *Anthology of Magazine Verse and Yearbook of American Poetry for 1979*; CG, 1980; *Poets in the South*, 1984.

Homestead: written Aug. 1-7, 1978; first published *Iowa Review*, Vol. II, No. 1, Winter 1980; CG, 1980.

Half Light: written 1978; first published *National Forum*, Vol. LX, No. 3, Summer 1980; CG, 1980.

Object: written June 25, 1978; revised Fall 1978; first published CG, 1980.

Hawks: written 1978; *Poetry on the Buses*, 1979; CG, 1980.

Scythia: written Fall 1978; first published *Maxy's Journal*, No. 3, 1979; CG, 1980.

Fence Shadows: written Fall 1978; first published CG, 1980.

Grist Mill: written Fall 1978; first published CG, 1980.

Cloud Climber: written Spring 1979; first published *The Missouri Review*, Vol. II, No. 1, Fall 1979; CG, 1980.

Notes for a Journey: written Summer 1972; first published *Pearl* (Denmark), No. 4, 1977; (in a somewhat loose form) *Cold Mountain Review*, No. 3, 1978; *Megacycles*, Vol. III, No. 2, 1978; CG, 1980.

Nasturtiums: written Summer 1972; first published *Poem*, No. 18, July 1973; CG, 1980.

Zinnias: written Summer 1972; first published *Poem*, No. 18, July 1973; CG, 1980.

Snapdragon: written Summer 1972; first published *Poem*, No. 18, July 1973; CG, 1980.

Silent Trade: written Summer 1972; first published *Poem*, No. 18, July 1973; CG, 1980.

Three Wishes: written Summer 1972; first published *Poem*, No. 18, July 1973; CG, 1980.

Counting the Grasses: written Fall 1978; first published CG, 1980; *The Kenyon Poets Anthology*, 1989.

Sassafras: written Fall 1978; first published CG, 1980.

The Fly: written Summer 1972; first published *Poem*, No. 18, July 1973; CG, 1980.

Dragonfly: written 1975; first published *Bits*, No. 7, Jan. 1978.

VII

Beggar From the Northern Shires: written 1954; first published *TCOL*, 1957; *Poets in the South, 1977-78.*

Conquistadores: written 1958; first published *BP*, 1962.

Quetzalcoatl: written 1952; first published *TCOL*, 1957.

News From Syracuse: written 1962; first published *The Listener* (U.K.), June 2, 1964.

The Earl of Arundel: written Summer 1972; first published *The Georgia Review*, Vol. XXVIII, No. 2, Summer 1974.

Quaker Ellwood: written 1978; revised 1987; first published *The Sewanee Review*, Vol. XCVII, No. 3, Summer 1989.

Wolsey: written 1987; first published *The Sewanee Review*, Vol. XCVII, No. 3, Summer 1989.

English History Poem: written Nov. 1969; first published *Outposts* (U.K.), No. 88, Summer 1971.

Portrait: written 1958; first published *BP*, 1962.

Reported Missing: written, Jan. 30, 1970; first published *Cold Mountain Review*, No. 3, Spring/Summer 1975.

To My Neighbor And Almost Namesake Shot By Strangers While Walking His Dog And Among His Flowers: written Spring 1975; first published *White Trash: An Anthology of Contemporary Southern Poets*, 1976.

Marianne: written 1972; first published *Poem*, No. 30, July 1977.

Valtellina, 1945: written Dec. 2-7, 1981; first published *The St. Andrews Review*, No. 26, 1983.

Dongo: written 1987; first published *New Virginia Review*, Vol. VI, 1988.

VIII

Crossing the Line: written 1975; first published *Poetry*, Vol. CXXIX, No. 6, Summer 1978; CG, 1980.

St. Andrew, North Shore: written Aug. 1976; first published *Canto*, Vol. II, No. 2, Summer 1978; CG, 1980.

Bathsheba: written Aug. 28, 1976; first published *Canto, Vol. II, No. 2, Summer 1978;* CG 1980; *The Prairie Wind*, No. 2, Fall 1992.

Road Junction North of Bridgetown: written Aug. 1976; first published *Canto*, Vol. II, No. 2, Summer 1978; CG, 1980.

St. Leonard's Churchyard, Bridgetown: written Aug. 1976; first published *Canto*, Vol. II, No. 2, Summer 1978; CG, 1980.

Rose Hall: written 1960; first published *Selection* (U.K.), Autumn 1963; *The Fiddlehead* (Canada), No. 71, Spring 1967.

Olive Trees: written 1954; first published *TCOL*, 1957.

Storm Over Lake Como: written May 1985; first published *The William and Mary Review*, Vol. 26, No. 1, Spring 1988.

Bergamo: written May 1985; first published *Tar River Poetry Review*, Vol. XXVIII, No. 1, Fall 1988.

In the Prague Botanical Gardens: written Sept. 8-13, 1988; first published *The Sewanee Review*, Vol. XCIV, No. 4, Fall 1991.

Laborer Near Ballinrobe: written May 1968; first published *Cold Mountain Review*, No. 3, Summer 1975.

Letter From St. Antonin Noble Val: written 1979; first published *Tar River Poetry Review*, Vol. XXVIII, No. 1, Fall 1988.

Nsangwini Cave Paintings: written 1986; first published *The Kenyon Review*, Vol. X, No. 2, Spring 1988; *North of Wakulla*, an Anhinga Anthology, 1989.

Thorn: Mlawula: written Nov. 19, 1985; first published *Kentucky Poetry Review*, No. 24, Fall 1988.

Y'iebo: written 1986; first published *The Kenyon Review*, Vol. X, No. 2, Spring 1988.

Mozambique: written Aug. 29-30, 1982; first published *Partisan Review*, Vol. LII, No. 3, Fall 1985.

Doubles: Malolotja: written Oct. 1985; first published *Caesura*, Vol. 1, No. 3, Spring 1986.

IX

In the Imperial Ballroom: written Fall 1975; first published *Poem*, No. 30, July 1977.

Alley of the Moon: written Summer 1976; first published *Poem*, No. 30, July 1977.

Chez Rat: written Sept. 1982; first published *American Literary Review*, Vol. 5, No. l, Spring 1994.

The Juggler: written 1955; first published *TCOL*, 1957.

The Leveller: written 1954; first published *TCOL*, 1957.

Oxford Street: written 1954; first published *TCOL*, 1957.

Anne Frank: written 1954; first published *TCOL*, 1957.

Defeat: written 1956; first published *TCOL*, 1957.

Thomas: written Dec. 1954 (Jerusalem); first published *BP*, 1962.

Country Priest: written 1953; first published *BP*, 1962.

In My Father's House: written 1991; first published *American Literary Review*, Vol. 5, No. 1, Spring 1994.

Simple Directions: written Sept. 22, 1992; first published *Visions*, No. 49, Fall 1995.

Ancient Piety: written 1970; first published *Mediterranean Review*, Vol. IV, No. 2, Winter 1971.

Marriage: written 1961; first published *Outposts* (U.K.), No. 49; *BP*, 1962.

Moonwort, Money Plant, or Honesty: written 1975; first published *CG*, 1980.

Three Nursery Rhymes: written 1958; first published *BP*, 1962.

Catalan: written 1981; first published *The Missouri Review*, Vol. 3, No. 1, Fall 1983.

Messenger from Fez: written Feb. 26, 1984; first published *Cairn*, No. 20, Spring 1984.

Jewish Festival: written 1959; first published *The Listener* (U.K.), May 24, 1962; *BP*, 1962; *Poets in the South, 1977-78*.

Et Incarnatus Est: written 1954; first published *TCOL*, 1957.

Lazarus: written 1955; first published *TCOL*, 1957.

Mystic: written 1954; first published *TCOL*, 1957.

Dove: written Oct. 1954; first published *TCOL*, 1957.

The Dust of Avila: written 1975; first published *Poem*, No. 30, July 1977.

Chameleon: written Fall 1971; first published *Three Rivers Review*, No. 5, Spring 1972.

Sans: written 1969; first published *American Literary Review*, Vol. 5, No. 1, Spring 1994.

Letters to Demetrius: written June 28, 1981; first published *Sidewinder*, Spring 1984.

X

Circe and Her Lovers: written Feb. 1973; first published *Poetry*, Vol. CXXIII, No. 1, Oct. 1973; *UNICORNS*, 1976; *Poets in the South, 1977-78*.

The Danaides: written 1966; revised 1969; first published *Poetry*, Vol. CXVI, No. 1, April 1970; *UNICORNS*, 1976.

Artist in Wartime: written 1970; first published *The Georgia Review*, Vol. XXV, No. 1, Spring 1971.

War: written 1953; first published *TCOL*, 1957.

Graphic by Fritz Pauli: written Oct. 25, 1973; first published *Hanging Loose*, No. 26, Winter 1975; *CG*, 1980.

March: written March 1968; first published *The Transatlantic Review*, No. 35, Spring 1970.

Footnote to Homer: written 1975; first published *Poem*, No. 30, July 1977.

Ballad of the Rain: written 1955; first published *TCOL*, 1957.

For Wilfred Owen: written Summer 1970; first published *The Dalhousie Review* (Canada), Vol. 53, No. 1, Spring 1973.

Path Under the Medlars: written 1975; first published *Southern Poetry Review*, Vol. XVI, No. 2, Fall 1976; *White Trash: An Anthology of Contemporary Southern Poets*, 1976; *Poets in the South, 1977-78*; *CG*, 1980.

Carnival in Time of Plague: written 1987; first published *The Sewanee Review*, Vol. XCVII, Vol. 3, Summer 1989.

Evening in Ferrara: written 1989; revised 1990; first published *Lullwater Review*, Vol. II, No. 2, Spring 1991.

Snake: written Spring 1972; first published *The Seneca Review*, Vol. 4, No. 1, May 1973; *The Scotsman* (U.K.), Oct. 20, 1973.

In Time of Plenty: written Fall 1974; first published *International Poetry Review*, Vol. 5, No. 1, Spring 1979.

To Margaret: written 1962 as the Dedication of *A Book of Pictures*; first published BP, 1962.

Epithalamion: written Aug. 3-4, 1983; first published *Kentucky Poetry Review*, Vol. XX, No. 2, Fall 1984.

Roads: written Sept. 1981; revised 1987; first published *Tar River Poetry Review*, Vol. XXVIII, No. 1, Fall 1988.

Amour Propre: Clarence: written Spring 1951; first published *TCOL*, 1957; *The Guinness Anthology* (U.K.), Number Two, Best Poems of 1957, 1958.

Don Juan in Winter: written 1967; revised 1973; first published *The Georgia Review*, Vol. XXVIII, No. 2, Summer 1974; *Keener Sounds: Selected Poems from The Georgia Review*, 1987.

Venice: written 1955; first published BP, 1962.

Bethany: written Aug. 25-28, 1976; first published *Poem*, No. 30, July 1977.

Gifts: written 1970; revised 1986; first published *America*, Dec. 19, 1987.

Introduction

It is presumptuous of me to be writing a brief introduction to this selection of the poems, old and new, by Michael Mott. He does not need my words, or, indeed, the words of any poet I can think of, to call attention to the impeccable quality, the excellence of his art and craft. His poems—line by line, stanza by stanza, group by group—speak for themselves, and they do so wonderfully well.

Presumptuous it may be, then, but it is also a pleasure and an honor to share with the reader of this book my own delight in Michael Mott's poetry. As a poet, myself, I have admired (and envied) Michael Mott's poems, without stint or reservation, for more than forty years. Our first books, his *The Cost of Living* and my *The Reverend Ghost* were both published in 1957, albeit at the time we were unknown to each other. I have followed his works, the steady, cumulative growth and development of 'his art with enthusiasm, learning something (as a poet) by his admirable example, rejoicing in his significant achievement. More to the point, as a demanding reader—and I do read a lot of contemporary poetry purely and simply as a reader who is ever eager to enjoy the delight and instruction that only poetry can offer—I have never been, in any way, disappointed. As a reader, I place him among a baker's dozen of living and working poets in our language who are truly masters, those precious few without whom our lives and our language would suffer irreparable injury.

I should also add that there are many contemporary poets, more than any baker's dozen, who, for one shabby reason or another, happen to be very well-known and much honored, but whose absence would honestly be no great loss either to the language or the tradition. One of the things I admire about Michael Mott, the man, is that he has in no way and at no time ever complained about the common injustices of the literary world, injustices that have allowed lesser talents to bask in the gaudy limelight of public attention and false reputation so characteristic of our end-of-the-century celebrity culture. It seems evident, considering the amount of work he has done, including several novels and the best-selling authorized biography, *The Seven Mountains of Thomas Merton* (1986), that Michael Mott has next to no time for negative thinking ,and feeling. He has spared himself, and us, from the tropes of unearned nihilism and massive self-pity so characteristic of much contemporary poetry. Clearly he has been too busy over all these years, year by year, creating poems of undiminished vigor and energy and undeniable integrity, and all of it without any loss or weakening of his extraordinary productivity or the least decline in the quality of his work. This is very rare. With some notable exceptions the history of poets is usually different. We grow old in spirit and performance even as our bodies age into enmity.

Consider the size and scope of this gathering, a book running 271 pages and according to my own rough count, presenting 235 poems (some of which are composed of several individual poems), poems of all shapes and sizes (forms), remembering that what we have here is a selection from his larger oeuvre, and taking note that though some poems are smaller and lighter than others, there is no falling off anywhere, that even the slightest epigram or the briefest lyric has earned and holds its appropriate place with the more intricate and complex meditations, narratives, and dramatic monologues. Bear in mind that, although there are both very early and very recent poems here, the book, itself, is organized (and very carefully so) by topics, and formal kinships rather than by chronology of creation or publication. Which means a couple of things at the least. First that, whether written early or late, these poems are now essentially simultaneous, that here and now are all together and are as fresh as if they were one and all written yesterday (and, in a real and critical sense, they were). That, secondly, though the poet, himself, inevitably will have grown and changed, matured in life and in his art, he has done so without losing the qualities with which he began his career. Most often artistic growth and development are accomplished by radical changes, often at the loss or, anyway, a distinct and observable turning away from one's original habits and strengths and interests and concerns.

In an autobiographical essay written for *Contemporary Authors Autobiography Series* (Volume 7), Mott tells the story of his first published poem, "Amour Propre: Clarence." Turn to page 268 of this collection and you will find that fine poem which stands with all the others, fits in perfectly with the larger structure of the book. Without the author's own accounting, not many, if any (I guess) would ever take it as his first published poem. It could easily have been written at any time during the forty-odd years since it first appeared. Which is not at all to say that the poet's work, his ways and means, has not changed since then. Quite the contrary, Michael Mott is in fact, a restless spirit, constantly driven, it seems, to try new and different and even daring things. But his work is happily inclusive. New developments, discoveries and directions have not required the closing of doors behind him. From the beginning, we can see now in this volume, he was not fumbling to find himself and his way, hit or miss, but already pointed in the way he has gone.

The qualities of Michael Mott's poems, the things which serve to define them as altogether his own, nobody else's, are paradoxical. In one sense, for example, he is a traditionalist. He demonstrates a rare mastery of metrics and of a wide variety of verse forms. The fingers of one hand count the living poets who can fairly be called his peers in prosody. Here you will find an amazing variety of verse forms, supple and fluent and unobtrusive. At the same time you will also find here a gracious plenty of prose poems, "experimental" poems (see, for example, the sequences of "Letters" and "Myths"), and superbly realized poems in free verse, all of these things gracefully united by the sharing of the poet's voice, partly, as Mott is, 20th century British, and partly, and deeply rooted as he also is in American history and the American experience. As Mott writes in his *Contemporary Authors* autobiographical piece, his American (and maternal) great-grandfather, from Maine, "led what must have been the last charge of the Civil War and won the Medal of Honor." The result of his divided inheritance is, among other things, a voice fully at ease with the whole range of our English language. It has also allowed him to write some of the finest poems ever written about the Civil War (see section V, "America, the Haunted Landscape"). With that unique voice, which, in truth comes to us in and through many voices, Mott creates characters of all kinds who speak for themselves.

There is also the great gift, the blessing of an ear with perfect pitch. There is a subtle and diverse music playing in all these poems, a rich virtuosity (occasionally elaborate) of end rhymes and internal rhymes, masculine and feminine, and echoes. The verbal texture of Mott's poems—that is, the complex relationship of the sound of the words to the things denoted by them—could serve as a textbook of brilliant examples. Read these poems aloud, paying close attention to the judicious punctuation or, as is sometimes the case, the complete absence of same.

Like all good poems, from Homer until here and now, these poems are meant to be music and need to be heard as well as seen on the printed page. But seeing, the visual and sensuous affective experience of the poem, is urgently important as well. No poet that I know of has used color as wisely and as well as Mott has. He has a trained painter's eye.

All of these things add up to what the reader can't fail to notice and appreciate—that these poems are the work of a greatly gifted poet possessing a mastery of technique, demonstrating that the ancient and honorable tools of the trade, handled by a sophisticated contemporary, are brightly renewed, shine like new-minted coins. But beyond that, beyond the absolutely essential and inseparable aesthetic surface, there are the subjects of these poems, what they are about, what, finally, they have to say to us and what, in that saying, in this particular show and tell, is the burden of Michael Mott's love affair and quarrel with the world. You will find that he is constantly sifting the shards of history, ancient and modern, examining historical characters and events from many angles and from variable distances. Just so he evokes and examines the myths, the fables and fairy tales that have ghosted us from the beginnings of time and poetry. In whatever form he is using, narrative, meditative, dramatic, there is also always a lyric poet standing close by in the shadows. There is always the tense possibility that any poems may suddenly burst into bloom. Which is only to say, as you will find for yourself, that the poems, in this arrangement, speak to and of each other. They are also freighted with allusive homage to the great books, especially the Bible and the Greeks, but likewise to the literature a civilized 20th century reader justly ought to have in his or her intellectual portfolio. Nevertheless (again the paradox) Michael Mott is not a "bookish" poet. Books, the stories they convey, are alive to him and come to life for the reader. Moreover he also writes (and interweaves these among the other poems) poems directly out of personal experience, occasional poems, elegies and love poems, poems close to the purity of song.

It was, as I said, presumptuous for me to begin this introduction and it is presumptuous to have gone on for so long when the great pleasure of the poems is all that really matters. But there is one more thing, one more quality of Michael Mott's poetry I should like to celebrate—his profound sense of place. This gift would be extraordinary enough if he had, like many good poets, settled on one place as his own homeplace. But Michael Mott is a widely traveled, traveling man. He has been all over and around the world—"Italy, Greece, Egypt, Lebanon, Jordan, Israel," he tells us in his autobiographical essay, also Africa. And he can summon up these places with accuracy, authenticity, and authority. England, of course, is home; but so is the United States where, all the way from the southwest to his favorite mountains and rivers of north Georgia, he is at once at home and an outsider rediscovering his heritage. Nobody else in my lifetime has written such moving and living landscapes in celebration of our huge, haunted country. Nobody else has made the names of our rivers and mountains, cities and little towns, and our half-forgotten battlefields so vividly his own.

—*George Garrett*

Woman and the Sea

I

"Flesh, voice, the enduring habit"

(The Persistence of Memory)

RED LEAVES

All that reading of Virgil one autumn in Georgia,
dogwood muscadine on a sky blue as blue paper.
What remains in my head now? Only a cry
of "Creusa!" "Creusa!" A name like my memory
sucked into stone holes, catacomb streets
of a sacked town, red lacquer of dogwood leaves.

Catcalls of Greeks after loot and women.
A Trojan remnant one woman short and Aeneas
risking father and son for his wife. Fire burnishes
bronze. Trash burns, red and black of the winedark
leaves. Trash, trash. And whatever the hand
moves to in panic. Flesh, voice, the enduring

habit, broken, betrayed in echo: "Creusa!" "Creusa!"
wind sport, distorted, unanswered, consonant leaves
sucked into holes of an endless alley. Boats
grind pebbles. At their oars the survivors
sing their first song of exile. Dawn over marshes,
wound open, a catastrophe of disturbed birds.

HARPSICHORD IN THE RAIN

Nothing to do these brown afternoons,
the bright van parked in the lane .
among Michaelmas daisies, the scarlet
postbox on the lichened wall.

Everywhere a brown blur of trees,
a white goose stepping out
over the steel plate slates—
never a wrong note.

These letters will be out of tune
before you are, playing Tallis,
where the black ivy drips pure drops
onto the spider's web between stones.

WOMAN AND THE SEA

imagine a whitewashed tower sea holly and a woman
contain in your ears the sound of the wind through
the three openings and doorway of the tower the returning
waves each third second on the pebbles also the rasp
of wind in the sea holly also the wind in the woman's
clothes an austerity of color imagine a gray day
think if you like of isolation or of Ilium
think if you like that she is thinking
she has walked from the bus from the station
think if you like of the lover she has left
or who has left her do not make too much of your thoughts
she will not walk into the sea there is a gravity of situation

whatever the sea may be in a dream a sentimental poem
or a colored print on a wall here it is simply the sea
a consoler perhaps but neither pathos nor tragedy
can be set on this stage a consoler by taking away
what even the Greeks would have left us not Sophocles
Aeschylus Euripides everything forced to some point
but the no point is nothing think if you like your own thoughts
that the woman is beautiful in a way that the calm
is not wholly deceptive that the light too is changing
pellucid one moment it is almost opaque at another
what is her lover to this and what are your eyes on the woman

burden the wind say it sighs say the sea holly catches
she must bend to untangle the hooks from the fringe of her dress
rub her leg with her fingers without looking down and afterwards
walk to the tower where she puts out her hands to the stones
she goes once round comes back to the doorway looks in does not enter

think if you like she is blind that she seeks out her cell
think if you like of her life in that small circulation
think of a question to ask ask are the three windows open important

she steps inside the tower and looks out through an opening of slates
and there is an island why an island now and never before
assuredly there is an island or at least a black rock in the water
what should there be there that is not there if we learn of an island

how long does she look at the rock and what thoughts come what thoughts
are beginning a while she comes out but what thoughts there to walk
so straight from the doorway without looking back and behind her
is falling each third second remember a wave of the sea and remember
especially remember I beg you the light and the wind she is walking in

WISTERIA

These vines and clusters round a door
that I maligned, whose one association
was with Victorian ladies faded
and their faded albums

What if a photograph brings back the vines
the clusters, you in that doorway?
I was unkind, both to those abstract ladies
and to us both who fade ... Oh

even to our album. They were more vigorous
than my trite mind—the living flowers
out of association, hung from no simple web
by your fair hair and in another hour

JUNIPER

sic et hominum multis fortuna sine flore est
— Pliny

It is late night, the unlighted side of leaves, I fumble with your name
as if some spell of mine where I am powerless could bring out of the waste
you thought you were, the everlasting winter of the evergreen, what you
were always waiting for. Impatient patience, as you felt the gathering
over and over—over and over knew the troubled start within of what
persuaded it would make the leap at last, out through the bars of branches
to the furthest points. Pruning each time the monstrous and monotonous
outgrowth of leaves to fall back to the root of things, to wait, to wait

right season. Are not all living things allowed not to be cursed for what
was blasted in their will? Hardest of all, what holds withholds to cry
richness of hope, perhaps, but poverty of luck. You had conceived your lack,
yet envied nothing, no one. Let that be said. It is no little thing.

How can I compensate, condone, console? I am no gardener grafting in the dark.
I bring you what you knew too well, bad luck, a poverty of words that will not
flower, except your pride refuse a gift no other has to give, accept
familiar failure as a kind of love that lives, for what it's worth,
on absences, out of all seasons, without roots or leaves or flowers.

ETRUSCAN MIRRORS

In these Etruscan mirrors—green
With the green clouds of age, another growing,
Like pools half-seen through a green spray, green branches,
Softening the forest glades in spring—
In these Etruscan mirrors once before
I saw those women of the long dark hair
And eyes serene and mocking,
Whose lips were brown and drawn
Like fruit already wounded ...
And when they came to speak, these leaning women,
Clouds formed, wind in the long dark hair,
Voices to silent laughter and the windfall lips
Parting to smile, smiles that stayed on half-seen,
While all the world within their mirrors
Turned to green.

POEM

I have in hand
The leaves that fell
Last Autumn,
That will fall again;
Green balls of moss
And two worn stones,
Scooped from the river bed.

I have the last
Of last year's corn—
Dusty and hard,
These ancient grains
Cling to my hair.

I walk in the low slanting rain
And at the weir
Watch where the swan's reflection runs
On the black waves.

I hear the lark's high note
And from a gorsebush pluck
Its feather now
To ornament my coat.

IN MEMORY OF WILLIAM STAFFORD 1914–1993

Ten minutes before dark
the swan flies down the lake
over the wine-dark autumn water
toward the dam and rush of water,
its wings tic-tac, its body
one line of white from beak
to feet. As Edward Thomas wrote:
"As if the bow had flown off
with the arrow."

That doe and unborn fawn
cleared from the mountain road
in Oregon have reached the
bottom of the canyon, and in
the prairie farmhouse, two
hundred miles from anywhere
on earth, the telephone
rings, rings, and now
no one on earth will answer.

THE SHEEP

This sheep was driven from the mountains
With all the flock, but it was different;
Under the outer wool were the knots,
Thousands of knots that could be read at the fort,
Making a spy's diary, the epilogue of a race,
Memories fast going out of the mind, and the great threat.

How should they name and number such a threat,
These two men in a room so far from mountains,
Scholar of knots and soldier of an alien race?
Whatever their answers, they are bound to be different.
The Captain prepares a punitive raid from the fort,
The scholar turns the diagrammed page, compares the knots.

Slowly, then fast, he explores the strands for more knots:
"We are undone, unaided. The threat
Winnows us daily. The false promisers keep to the fort.
Lost in this waste, forgotten, we are walled in by mountains.
Weather, disease, we bore before. This is utterly different.
Now, deserted by you, we go down, and what race

"Watches over the death of our race?
We are the last with the strength to tie knots
And the heart. We heard your words before. Now it's different,
This silence over the Pass, no one coming, the threat
Picking off one by one. Sniped at from mountains,
We think of *you*. What think you at the fort?"

The scholar's nails click in the wool at the fort.
In quiet he grows angry, a garrulous race!—
Sends for a second lamp, feels the chill from mountains.
The sheep presses closer. The knots
Speak no more of the threat.
He hunts as for lice, but this hunt is different.

Other messages now. Those who seem almost indifferent
To any besides themselves, ignore the fort,
Speak of their separation, more real than any threat:
Certain survivors apart from them, surviving the race,
As also their love, these who tied knots
Would reach for from mountains.

9

"This to you in the plain from me in the mountains.
We made plans before, but all this is different.
Do you remember when we needed no knots?
I promised you then to protect you better than a fort.
Our love won't help our race.
May it defend *you* still from any threat!"

"I do not fear the power of any threat;
Only I would have you beside me in the mountains.
You should not live away with an alien race,
Nor among any others alive, for we two were different.
There are no scented mosses down at the fort.
I cannot whisper now what I've lost in these knots."

The scholar looks up and shrugs. The knots
Speak of nothing. A kind of silence, a threat·
Perplexes the Captain, a desire to be quit of the fort.
He orders the column alert to be off to the mountains.
He is used to a riddle of sorts. This one is different.
He swears at all scholars, curses a baffling race.

They will be too late now to save any race.
Who but a fool would beg help in knots?
To whatever is left the soldier feels all but indifferent.
He marches to find and to quell the threat,
Wondering if mountain guns will work in these mountains.
He feasts with his men first. He sets forth from the fort.

Whatever happened elsewhere never reached the fort,
Not in time to save the sheep or to save the race.
It became history before the beast came out of the mountains,
Slow moving sheep, the carrier of the knots.
It was a sort of language and it failed. The threat
Came down alone to talk in the plain and that was different.

The sheep carried fear, itself indifferent
To whatever it brought. It bleated in the fort,
"Baa, baa." When it saw the knife it saw the threat.
But it died dumb, made mutton like all its race,
Spotted on slopes once like so many knots
Far in the hinterland of distant mountains.

Fort of language, spokesman of the race,
Indifferent echo of an oath, all its unravelled knots
Threat on the Captain's back. Cold wind in the mountains.

TARN

Tout ce qu'on donne fleurit,
tout ce qu'on garde pourrit.
— Maurice Utrillo

Sweetness and bitterness of rivers: Tarn,
Tamar, Aveyron, Chattahoochee, and a stream
on Canigou, I name you, sweetness and bitter-
ness of exile, a taste of salts and sulfur

each distinct, as if the essence of the stone
flowed in their water only, left the stone
no more a stone than the ghost shells
of certain insects, long outgrown, that cling

by their ghost fingers to dry stalks. What's
gone out of everything outgrown, out of rooms
flowing through open windows into streets
like this one? Montauban, red city by a

tawny river, what love of mine was ever so distinct
it left its essence on the air? I mean to taste
the wind whenever the wind turns, an emptiness
between old buildings where ten thousand Sundays

crumble the pink brick and the blistered shutters.
Red city of dead martyrs, who died perhaps with eyes
watching the Tarn, the traffic, meaning to ask
the meaning. In any given moment what we hold onto rots.

THE DEFEAT OF NAMES

The burden of the blood, romantic tale,
From what red cave, my tyrants, did you carry
Such blocks of porphyry, or lease those hunting streams
Downhill, across dull countrysides that carried
So far afield, St. Christopher, upon your back, Columbus,
Off to Americas of Aztec gold and pampas,
Or all those bird-crazed days the slavers married
Their Ham-black Bibles with the bride-white islands?

Shall I set fingers to those formal grooves?—
Sharp names in gothic choirs, softer by orchards,
Oh, overgrown, gray quilted, where one apple
Burns, lamp of winter, at this chapel bare, and Eden
Is over one more stream, perhaps in Pyder—
Lanherne, that holy vale, if Mawgan buried
A grail of primrose and soft moss and granite,
Where, wearing silk hats, poets searched for Idylls—
These other worlds, Gawain, these star-mad islands!

Some summer day across long lawns the arrows pointed
(The names then rested in their pleasant nests, none singing),
The tallest oak tree missed, targets went spinning,
Streamers through peas and beans. Tigers in bamboo cages
Growled like lost water, voices broke free from laurel,
Doves fell like soot and snow, rooks built their arks from shipwrecks,
Bells dragged up metal from the corn-drowned valley ...

> Then Adam drinking by the front steps saw
> The trees all bore his daughters' names
> And at the white gate figures dressed in flames ...

Letters come asking for the price of shoes for children
Off in America. Fever took some. A bullet
Carried the flag from Bunker Hill. Another
Rode up the Rio Grande with his wife and child upon his saddle,
Two days he rode; and when he died in Maine long after
Two days he rode again to bring their bodies
Back from the flood's lair, from the sun's black sowing.
Perhaps he married her again that night in Texas,
Danced to the fiddles in the greening water ...

So round the loft of wax the moth goes,
And the lighthouse,
Besieged by birds all night,
And in the morning,
Rises from birdglass in a glittering Arctic …

Down in the book at last, privateer, lawyer,
Protester, maker of pianofortes, coalman, merchant,
Seller of wines—so many cherrystones I might have threaded,
Bubbles poised on the drop of that Niagara,
Such salmon spawn of hope, each one survivor
Of what enormous wars, what massacres, what chances;
Fractions defeated all but him, on each side thousands
Fell, every bit as just, when up to daylight
He stormed alone, each jack-king to his castle,
Claiming his earth, bread, water, pain and name.
Yet here, what hold?—skies black with bats and starlings—
That abacus of names. Sometimes a headstone
Lasts forty years before it goes to make a wall. So,
Come influence or kings, such revolutions
Tumble the brave, just, beautiful, meek,
Oh in a cold bed. Oblivion. Rain frets
The carved rill, ornate angel, solid cross.
Not long for immortality, 'immortelles',
Or in a jamjar thrust like a wasptrap the browning dandelions.
Moss, softer than rain, breaks stones, dulls
The crown and steeples of the best cut names. Also
Paint peels on the stern of a rowing-boat set to commemorate
Two men and one boy found frozen
Upon this beach . . .

Upon this beach: oiled guillemot, cork float, albatross, amber …

Most poems are about love today—or, tomorrow remember?—
How little stays, how strange the changes.

Plucking your counterpane, ashamed of mortality,
You pull the threads through from behind, break off the recording
Of Wilde at a Shakespeare Reading, banish the sunlight
From a wall of the Villa Medici; repack a hamper
In an Alpine valley; peel away labels, Colombo, Sakkara,

Close doors on the Gainsboroughed rooms, give notice to gardeners,
Bury a lifetime of pets—and when Ginger is lifted
From the end of your bed, you shy the last time from the memory
Of a nurse who hid cats in the bedclothes to terrify children.
Diminished in mirrors that glimpse of Medusa. Remote as Eurydice,
A red-headed spectre retires down a darkening corridor.
And now through the sunlight instead steps old Nan with her walking stick,
Striking the heads of the flowers that will roost in her hat.

Already you lie under stone in the rain and the red blur of buses—
Lie among Bletchingley dead and the castaway dead of da Cunha,
Already I reach back for that and already find nothing.
Nothing for you. For myself only so much forgotten.
One thing I recall without wanting it, how your head at the end
Made me think of King Seti's mummified head ... how I wanted
To find something of beauty in that—and somehow succeeded.

No one is crying our names anymore over islands;
No one sings us to sleep with our own, or pretends—without heirs—
We leave floating around us the rings of another Titanic to save us
Out of green seas, or from iceworlds forming, breaking off,
Sliding down from both Poles in the night to o'erwhelm us.

Yet even the drowned have their coral, their key to the kingdom.

II

THE LETTERS

(The Creation of Myth)

"G-d drew them [THE LETTERS],
hewed them, combined them,
weighed them, and through them
produced the whole creation and everything
that is destined to be created."

– *The Sefer Yetshirah*, or Book of Creation

THE LETTERS I

How A came first when THE LETTERS waited

Some were too forward. They were put back
Some made up the syllables of Death
They came after

Some made up together the name of Justice
They were hidden in the middle

"If it is the world you seek there can be no justice
and if it is justice you seek there can be no world"

These letters were mingled
that the world might be made

How great A came before all and how it was spoken
Aleph and Alpha
of the two tribes
of the oxen and the axes

How it held up the world in a hundred aspects
How one of these
was the Titan Atlas

And how Chaos cried out against A
It was the first taking

How the teacher spoke sternly the letter A to the children
and how the sages smiled at his emphasis

Without A, where were we?
In the erasing of the scroll
we were the fine shavings of sheepskin
Mercy and Love were not
Death, first, there might be, or Justice

MYTHS I

In the beginning

we are assured there was a garden
palisaded   PARADISE
                (from the Persian)
with a white horsehair
of water
ascending
         in the heat

AZIMUTH and ZERO
                (from the Arabic)
on the hottest days

as in Italian gardens still
             white marble
             dark trees

against the glare
there was water
             Primal matter
and the sound of water
and the echo of water
             the tumbling of doves
             and their converse
             in accord

————Where did the water come from?

————It was the let of stones
             and it is present
             smaller
             more lively
             than the eye of a pigeon
             in the hardest flint

————How came the water before the stone?

————It was there before the stone
             and the stones came to guard it
             but stones also were of water once
             was not paradise palisaded?

There was petrification even in paradise
It enclosed the zero

MYTHS II

"And such was the intensity of the heat that many were
turned into glass, together with the finer matter about them"

> Question: Was this fable or fact?
> STORY or HISTORY having the same root in Greek
> "A TRUE HISTORY" or "A TRUE STORY"—see
> translations of Lucian

Yet imagine it—
turned into glass

of what color?

Assume the predominate color was blue
the color of darkness visible
the second light of the candle of Cabbalah
and also the robes of the bards were blue
worshippers of Andraste, goddess of the Druids

Let us take blue for the ground
and a cast of purple
blue bottle glass of the sea
and of the Virgin of Guadalupe
in Mexico

People of blue glass
outlasting those of grass
of dust
of A-dam
red clay

but co-equal in eternity
with those of volcanic dust
at Pompeii

and at Hiroshima
there were only shadows

If I am to speak of
metamorphosis
or metempsychosis

——and the dolls of Dresden

"Horrible to think of it"
                              Virgil

and more horrible
surely
to accept a part in it

Those living in an era of
such metamorphosis
should not throw anything

"Metamorphoseos wot what I mene"
says Chaucer's Man of Law

and where is the law now?
only mutability

Alchemical change of men

The true lights of G-d
in Gnosis
Marcion for one

scattered, fragmented

children of blue glass
saints in crystal

Let us assume anything

In history is all story
and the splinters
of manglass

MYTHS III

What stirred the dust?——

What stirred the dust?
the worm

as the wind stirred
the laurel leaves

The earthworms remake the Earth
many times over
in each generation

it is not man
but the worm
that remakes Earth

who shall discover
such greatness?

It is sealed in silence
and a man studies himself

MYTHS IV

Was there a woman before Eve?

Before Eve there was the
idea of women
and it touched the Earth

It was not Lilith
but a rumor
nameless

A woman goes into her house
Eve is here
and the hours of Eve

but the nameless is still
unnamed
and the Earth
expectant

MYTHS V

How shall we tell eternity in a ring?
and Alexander stood here
and Hitler there?

And if it be the rings of a tree
the tree is upon the ring
and the blade of the axe in the earth

and if it be the rings in water
shall they outlast
the sound of the falling stone?

The sound of the stone
will outlast its fall
going into another stone
which is within the ring

and if no man can hear it
what then?

We are near the beginning of things
and the sounds of the Battle of Actium
are in the waves still

MYTHS VI

How animals may be lured by a sweet smell
is a pretty trick
and the matter of many theses

but though everyone knows how a unicorn may
be taken
there is no captive unicorn
to prove the success of the experiment

not—let us be charitable—
for lack of virgins, or mirrors, or combs
only for lack of unicorns

Yet who is to say
that the absence of unicorns
has not been a greater thing
than the presence of lions?

It is the sweet smell of the unicorn
that has lured men

How tactful this test of
virginity
not of maidens only
but of the most refined scholars

This is a long tower of ivory
that shines
in the moonlight

And a man may lack
musk, or civet, or rosewater

and grow mad of love
on an absence of unicorns

MYTHS VII

"Some of the diseased hold themselves like dead
and others believe they are of glass"

——so Conrad of Magenberg on diseases of the spleen

And there have been young girls also
in the time of adolescence
who believed they were turning
by hours before the glass into glass
undone by ambition
and by their imagination also

Others thought themselves lifted aloft
by rocs from remote mountain valleys of Arabia

set in portions of meat
thrown down
by the devious hunters

and were recovered
Shamirs
or diamonds

unbreakable lights
though lidded
until the cutters
of polyhedra
in polyhedra
created them eyes

so they became in themselves
moving starmaps

infinite changing
manifestations
of fire
on the dark foilcloth
of nights

But the more brittle sick
feared everything

the least jar or
collision
of the bed they lay in
or the hands of the nurse

being not diamonds
but common glass

that the kiss of a loved one
might shatter

a fallen spoon
or even
the accident
of their own breathing

These reflected nothing
from a mass of bedclothes

only the fear of touch
a glazing of terror

MYTHS VIII

"Peace to the beaver," says the writer of
The Flowers of Virtue

And indeed this creature has much honor
in all bestiaries
who being hunted for his testicles
which were needed in medicine
emasculated himself
and so went free
and the hunters in health
and in profit
drank to the beaver

Honor the beaver
but what is this virtue?

Beast and man
should die as they were made
even a priest
—though not one of Cybele's

Peace at too high price

Beast and man—
we should be tempted as we were made
It is our honor to wear the days
and nights out in turmoil
—excepting the Stoics

Of love and lust there is plainly no cure
but time or the teeth of the beaver

THE LETTERS II

————What were THE LETTERS doing?

They were behind the letters
the little letters before the great

in Xhosa
in Zuni
in Kymric
in cant
in gabble

In the play of the ballad
also in the sermon

They crowded the line
like swallows
no tail angled the same
They were alone like a fly
shining on a gatepost

They were an anthill disturbed
They were hornets erupting forth

They were tsi tsi
They were Moog Moog

They were bath-kol
They were Maa-mar

In microphones they were magnified
They whispered softly
in autophones
through the windpipes of cranes

On the seabed and in the hurricane
they crackled
they crowed and spoke

They stalked the hills
They slept in sealed chambers
They danced in the rings

They were as sibilant
as a snake in dry leaves
They fractured like a fall of tiles

They were Arum Arum
They were nu'voo nu'voo

They hung on both sides of the head
like beards
like twin swarms of bees

They buried their dead
They escaped in excelsior

They were erased
They clapped hands in the flames

They were unraveled by moths
The silverfish licked them with its tail

They bred like a banquet of worms
They lay in levels like ten Troys

They ran fast together
they were a starling pack
they were a press of minnows
they were tadpoles
they were live writing
on the bed of streams

They were set together
in a bed of lead

They were dished from the printer's tray
They were scrambled by devils

They assumed importance
They undid their doing
They honored an oath
They broke their word

They were erased
They formed fours and conquered

They were all and nothing
they were only the letters
before THE LETTERS

Largest and least
they made up the telling of men

MYTHS IX

How one of the sages heard a bird singing
inside the tomb of a king
is a riddle not easy to be answered

for the tomb was of stone and in
eloquent footnotes he assures us
there was no crack in the sides
and the slab was in place

We cannot conjecture a cricket
out of the text
for the plain sense of the word
is bird
Nor would a hidden spring
account for the sound
nor some trick of the wind

How a bird could live enclosed in a tomb
and why it should sing there
we have no answer for

Yet the sage was not old
nor at fault upon other occasions

In discourse on the spleen of the wren
or in the method of resting by seabirds
he follows the correct models

In authority and observation
he is hardly to be bettered
while his follower
Anthony
tells of his master's delight
in the drumming of quails

One so scrupulous elsewhere
cannot be held to account
for an error of fact

yet the strangeness remains

MYTHS X

In the month of Athyr
when the leaves sleep
after their restlessness
when the rains
press on one another
like lovers
when the waters are mingled
the greater waters
and the least
when the eaves
and the gutters
are full of singing
when the black rat
slides by the river
when the stubble
is furred
when men walk
with their heads down
when they carry their clothes
like houses
like little homesteads of safety
like snails

MYTHS XI

And the tree by the water

Excepting all who passed
and did not stop to see

how many yellow blossoms in its boughs
how many glistening branches in the winter
how many birds

————nothing was always there

And the tree by the water

Excepting all who passed
and stopped but did not see

how its bark ran with rain
how close it came to trailing in the water
those furthest leaves
how water rose at times to meet it

————nothing was always there

And the tree by the water

Excepting all who saw
but did not see

And the tree by the water
The tree by the water

It was not Zion we lamented
It was our exile
from our very lives

MYTHS XII

"What is glass but still water?"
——so Jarry

Very still

It is the breaking of surfaces
that excites expectation
as in bathing in a still sea
there is recognition
that eras
are about to pass out of the blood

unrealized realization
there is division yet
no simple matter of skin

And in Venice
where glass is made
near a quiet sea
the palaces
blown from the feet of palaces
are almost perfect

where there is a flaw
it is a mere bubble

Easy to extend ourselves
at least by appearances
to sense the blood growing cooler
to enter
by the marine second door of palaces

Where is the flaw?

What is a bubble but air?

What do the glass blowers
blow around us?

What is it goes with us always
when we pass through surfaces
with our surfaces?

MYTHS XIII

And both ascend
two themes together
separate
and intertwined

the voices
of Tristan
and Isolde

or hawks
soaring
clockwise
and anti-
clockwise
over the valley
of the Harle

their marriage rings
made in the air
one circle
on another

or Chambord stair

three examples
in which the one
is sprung out of the earth
upon the counter moving
spiral
of the other

and each sustained there
in the perilous air

only in revolutions
of the opposite

ADAM NAMES
THE PRECIOUS STONES

Afa
Bak
Cof Abor As
Dja
Eis
Fazma
Gamrak
Hiop
Illor
Ja Asp Ja
Kissac
Lut
Mar Jid Esp
Noio Nag Noio
Ovvbakram
Pazur
Quijo Iod
Rubuzril
Sammansar
Totfeyrak
Ul
Vagasvag Shem
Waa Kepsur
Xuxus
Yitjuf
Zimats

ADAM NAMES
THE ANIMALS

Ac
Bez
Cuf
Di
Eop
Faw
Ginzal
Hut
Ipoth
Ji
Koz
Letlak
Mutal
Nepsa
O
Petzut
Quegor Upta
Rabu
Samsa
Tuton Obi
Ul
Vetzma
Wyst
Xtor Aa
Yu
Zept

MYTHS XIV

As Lucian: "Amber and the swans
have made me eloquent
upon all subjects"

As to the doorman answered Lugh:
"A poet I, I come from Appled Eamhain
of swans and yewtrees"

Under the bow of a bridge
in apple breathing autumn
yewtrees for foil
bright beads of amber
about their bodies sail
white and repeating white
the swans
of words, of eloquence

MYTHS XV

How apples were so often passwords
how they were magic to Merlin and many others
how the Field of Apple Trees was the Place of Presence in the *Zohar*
and how the king came to Avalon, the Isle of Apple Groves
to be restored after the grievous hurt at Camlann

How angels thirsted for the fruit of apples
and how the applespray makes marriages in heaven
and how the Rood was made of applewood
how Adam's seed was with the seed of apples
in secret store so many dark years in the cave

How the seed hangs in chambers like a lamp
how the spur shoots of apple trees bear flowers
how apple blossom frenzies men as well as moths
and yet how apples are the antidote for love

All these are mysteries beyond the text
Wisdom in apples who shall pare away?

THE LETTERS III

——What were THE LETTERS doing?

In Lucian, in Rimbaud's *Voyelles*
they paraded, they showed
their ways

in the *Correspondances* of Baudelaire
gracefully
gratefully
they accepted echoes

In the translations
of translations
in the hear-say
of hearsay

their shapes were shadows
they were weighed like weights
they lost their salt, their savor
they were like stoppered vials
they were like glassy bones
they were like white statues

In the rings
they were revenants

In the uniformity of type
they were the ghosts of voices

In the plainness of their end
they were the little letters
they diminished to a dot

MYTHS XVI

They were talking about stones
about the properties and holiness of stones

of Gervais of Tilbury and many others
Hebrews and Arabs
who had studied stones

In the afternoon
when the motes climbed in the sunlight
they were talking together about stones

about the turquoise sensitive to men's ills
about the amethyst that cures drunkenness
about the alsarik that heals eyes

In the afternoon
when the throat of the ostrich melts the gold
they were talking together about stones

MYTHS XVII

"I began to learn a new alphabet and meditate on words that
        hissed and words that gasped"

——so said Jerome, and there are many alphabets

How many alphabets?—of the oxen and the axes?

What syllables the thunder spoke and the water
and the hammer among the rocks
the camel and the jackal
what Attis said to Attis among the pinetrees
and the voice breathing in the cedars after Babel

Many alphabets and many tongues
yet each tongue matched to a little piece of earth
Adam, Adamah, Adam Kadmon—
of the red clay
or of the white
of crystallite, of ochre, of cinnabar
in the geology and geography of tongues after alphabets
and before alphabets

Define it downward
Is it not the pietas of a few fields
an unknown allegiance
as the water of a certain well is known
and the wine of a particular acre?

"O Taste and See"—
Is it not the abracadabra of the roots
and what nourishes the roots—
as the farmer first crumbles the loam
and after, the grainhead in his hands?

Is it not also the overcast of exile
the many accents of exile?
And who is not learnéd in leaving?

Lingua franca and Shibboleth of the earth
of the race and of every removal

ADAM NAMES
THE STARS

Azlahim
Besuur
Chafchas
Dunihhaboz
Es Os Es
Fetf
Germaznut Babil
Hasmasos
Iffafalur
Jomachai
Kimah Hamar
Lyahorabin
Muxust Isus Ior
Neyomar Abar
Ottixoxos
Pezragil
Quem Raffeen
Rymihoassam
So Amahal
Tukoorak Assur
Unffa Esparosin
Vobbehar
Wessesibbi
Xhorizames
Yesutza
Zibossamoxibistar

ADAM NAMES
THE FLOWERS AND TREES

Ap Uris
Balaffa
Cyomunda
Daxeyiis
Eiopia
Fii
Geomar
Hybor Eznabor
Ipylis
Jayomynthos
Kastrabel
Lynthelysum
Mar
Nixypys
Op Ramp Aiy
Pastrapel
Querror
Razwaxtzelen
Spasippi
Tor
Ubrellmar
Vad As Falla
Wo
Xasffyon
Yexta Aklagor
Zytheris

MYTHS XVIII

Wise was the sage
who told the man maddened with fear
by his own shadow
to study light

Yet no Dives, nor even
a poorer citizen
who had breakfasted
would know

how the first color
seen upon a day
after long fasting
may mend the spirit
for a while
or grow so terrible
inside the head

no study of the light
could put it right

MYTHS XIX

How Ulysses answered to No-name
and how Tristan
feigning madness
answered King Mark
"My father was an old hack
and my mother a ewe"

How No-name prospered
and how the disguised Tristan
butted the king's ewe

How Nemo invisible
walks in and steals
wine from the cup
cake from the platter
and then goes off to Nowhere
when the found thieves hang
under the trees
like seedpods

How the Have-names held a conference
and how Absent was chosen
How the Unknown Knight
taunted Sir Dinadan
How Anonymous went first
in the Anthology
and how It ravaged a country
and blew dust at the challenger

How All-in-All
outsmarted Solomon
and how she-she and he-he
bedded down in the marketplace

How Know-Nothing blamed Nobody
How the scholars argued over "ex Nihilo"
How the schools were divided, "Nemo" and "Nullus"
How mere nothing became Sir Somebody
and how often he regretted it
How the goddess responded to no one
and was worshipped by everyone

How the trees were name tagged by the Botanist
and how they remained rooted
How there was no river called Danube or Rhine
How the sea resisted Canute
And how love languished for the naming

——How all love went out in the wake of the name
like the riddle in unriddling

MYTHS XX

Consider the Aleut Indians
their alphabet of hunger

In a little while
a is in absence
b in the beaks of seabirds
c in cutwater and crags
d in dreams of the feast

How close the hills come
How sharp are stones

After so many days
the stomach turns on itself
the gnawing of the wolf
the whittling of whalebone
the strain of a windlass

Then a membrane is pinched
nail comes in under nail
awl punches sailcloth
and the spirit speaks
as iron balks
at a knot in hardwood

How soon thereafter
all this is forgotten
The huge appetite of pain
abated, goes elsewhere

nothing is near
no moss now fragrant

What is left of the head
praises privation
without words worships
the grown god Hunger

MYTHS XXI

"Souls do not sleep like dormice"

——so Raleigh

Indeed, but no soft thing at rest
without a shell

——Tread on the eggshells, angels

No pin
without unnumbered seraphim

What is secret of secret
will not anatomize

Disturb even a seed sleeping
and you harvest stones

For the old emblematist
the World Fire sleeps in a flint

Not Prometheus his fennel
carries a greater threat—

not an atom without—

That was some Great World
hidden, yet
anatomized!

But who shall probe the atom of atoms
out of its shell?

Who shall awake the soul sleeping its sleep?

Not Descartes find it in a gland
nor Boyle
in a drop of dew

Each generation renumbers the stars
Given as many generations
shall they reach the sum?

No pin
without unnumbered seraphim

——Tread on the eggshells, angels

Infinite secret mansions
where the soul coils in

MYTHS XXII

Even as the light going declares the darkness
So there was no sure knowing
Not anywhere sharp as a shadow
Absence assured the outline only

Even as sickness discovered every part
Not for a map the terra incognita
Displace of space
Near weight of unseen bodies

What ghosts believe in ghosts believe in—
Only without you there, said Strindberg
Was even madness real enough to bear

MYTHS XXIII

The tale tells how the letter T was in touch
and in Tristan falling from the tower
and how the lepers clutched at Isolde

What song sang Tristan in the air
seeing the sea so far below
and the surf like a scarf
how many times it came back on the sea's arm
and how the birds flew forward and back
beneath Tristan

when he saw the sun shine on the rocks
like the yellow points of the broom
when he touched the air
and not Isolde?

What were the sea mews calling in his ear
as he fell so far
so many minutes in the air?

He anticipated the sea
He felt cold come into his bones

He touched the foreland and the bay
With five fingers he caressed all Cornwall
With five he stroked the Forest of Morois
and with five the forest of the sea

He lay over the iron shadow
of Lethowstow, lost Lyonesse
as he had lain over Isolde

The tale tells how he escaped
that he sat naked on a rock in the middle of the sea
and he laughed outright:

"How to tell you, Cymry, of a lover's leap
How to tell you!"

And what song sang Isolde among the lepers
their skin against her skin
the plump of her white arm
in the hooks of their fingers?

How they clutched at the Queen
not fire so urgent
not the embrace of Tristan

and her marrow ached
under the skin, within the bone

"Is there another love, my love
the love of the hawthorn for the snow
the love of a stake for the winter sea
the love of the Man in the Moon?

"Is there another love, my love
the loved flesh for the fallen
the body beloved in a pelt of pain?

"And after this company
will you find me whole?
Will even I know my Eve's skin
from the thorn and the foliage?

"Will I leave our bed for the Moon
for the wolf-tones of briar?"

Truth ruthless in touch
So for a season is broken
the old spell
the enduring thing
like a sword
like a word misspoken
by air, by a lazar's hand
parted the lovers
the most faithful of lovers

ABACAZA

abacadaeafagahaiajakalamanaoapaqarasatauavawaxayaz

<table>
<tr><td></td><td>color</td><td></td><td>match</td><td></td></tr>
<tr><td>sound match</td><td>a</td><td>as</td><td>in</td><td>smell match</td></tr>
<tr><td></td><td>b</td><td>as</td><td>in</td><td></td></tr>
<tr><td></td><td>c</td><td>as</td><td>in</td><td></td></tr>
<tr><td></td><td>d</td><td>as</td><td>in</td><td></td></tr>
<tr><td></td><td>e</td><td>as</td><td>in</td><td></td></tr>
<tr><td></td><td>f</td><td>as</td><td>in</td><td></td></tr>
<tr><td></td><td>g</td><td>as</td><td>in</td><td></td></tr>
<tr><td></td><td>h</td><td>as</td><td>in</td><td></td></tr>
<tr><td></td><td>i</td><td>as</td><td>in</td><td></td></tr>
<tr><td></td><td>j</td><td>as</td><td>in</td><td></td></tr>
<tr><td></td><td>k</td><td>as</td><td>in</td><td></td></tr>
<tr><td></td><td>l</td><td>as</td><td>in</td><td></td></tr>
<tr><td></td><td>m</td><td>as</td><td>in</td><td></td></tr>
<tr><td></td><td>n</td><td>as</td><td>in</td><td></td></tr>
<tr><td></td><td>o</td><td>as</td><td>in</td><td></td></tr>
<tr><td></td><td>p</td><td>as</td><td>in</td><td></td></tr>
<tr><td></td><td>q</td><td>as</td><td>in</td><td></td></tr>
<tr><td></td><td>r</td><td>as</td><td>in</td><td></td></tr>
<tr><td></td><td>s</td><td>as</td><td>in</td><td></td></tr>
<tr><td></td><td>t</td><td>as</td><td>in</td><td></td></tr>
<tr><td></td><td>u</td><td>as</td><td>in</td><td></td></tr>
<tr><td></td><td>v</td><td>as</td><td>in</td><td></td></tr>
<tr><td></td><td>w</td><td>as</td><td>in</td><td></td></tr>
<tr><td></td><td>x</td><td>as</td><td>in</td><td></td></tr>
<tr><td></td><td>y</td><td>as</td><td>in</td><td></td></tr>
<tr><td>taste match</td><td>z</td><td>as</td><td>in</td><td>touch match</td></tr>
</table>

MYTHS XXIV

What was the song of Arthur in his sadness?

"Bitter the frost, bitter the tree, bitter the stone
bitter the white wave of the sea
that in this island
men should be born so mean"

Roebuck, badger, and raven
What song sang Bran's head
as it swung in the wind?

"Bitter the bread, bitter the wine, bitter the company
of those who come after

"If the windows on old grief are open
what comfort is kept
in the little house of winter
in barton, hanger, and coombe?"

Dogfox, lapwing, and salmon
What song sang Merlin in the maiden's rock?

"Better the silence, better the wind in the thorns
What treasure if letters lie loreless?
What craftspell endures in the earth?

"What profit the old leaves lost
to a plot green as parsley
old tales of serpents and moons
or the Babel of waves far off?"

MYTHS XXV

All the Proud Walkers

Were they stars
or pilgrims?

"Here and Everywhere"
their motto

with staff
and scallop shell

like the samara
winged seed of the elm
blown by the world's wind
across the world

Time is the outward aspect
of Eternity

"The little owl
upon the eaves
watches the sun go down"
——so Virgil

One sun, one journey
here and everywhere

MYTHS XXVI

How they came to Killiwic
the old and the young
under the circles
of the buzzard hawks

Green wheat marked out the ramparts
the fosse was of dark briar

The flint with its sealed flame
blocked the ear of the warrior

A child could count the spirals on its fingers:

> ONE as in those very fingers
> TWO as in the coiled beast sleeping
> THREE as in the gold ring of the sea princess of Tyre
> FOUR as in the castle of Arianrhod
> FIVE as in the cross section of a young apple tree

and there were many more

How many more?

As many as the puzzle in a children's book—
counting the faces in the foliage

Who picks up the thread of the maze
never walks straight

Who takes up the riddle of the dance
dances in eight

Who comes by different levels in the latter day
is never late

neither a second Dylan by the track of green
nor any other Merlin by the briar

BUT WHAT IS

"But what is Paradise? All things that are ... save
one tree and the fruits thereof ..."

By the dark glass and the clear
what shall be prophesied of Paradise?

One shadow overall
of the tree
       like a mighty river
Fruit in the skin of fruit
forever remembered   as once
under the rind   and always

             all seasons and everywhere
             shared

THE LETTERS IV

——What were THE LETTERS doing?

They were laughing among themselves

——Were they like actors in the wings?

No, they were like children
even the terrible ones

They had no mind to men
They were not even laughing at men

They were mocking each other—
their colors and shapes
their scents and sounds

They were miming and mimicking
the taste of S
the texture of L

They were somersaulting and dancing
They were trying on disguises
They were waiting for new worlds

III
Lessons Are the Least We Learn.
(The Myth Enters the World.)

PROTEUS

Long ago, as you guessed,
I sold out for mere possibility,
bartered character for change,
discovered everything but myself.

Now my marvelous memories
are not mine. I can claim
nothing. I lost what little I had
in taking notes. The photographs lie.

I can remember much—not the
color of eyes or a name,
one girl simply became another, one
city ... Being a seal or a halcyon

never helped. I was lost in my skin,
feathers, scales, that terrible emptiness.
I give back now what the sea gives
or a grave: an amphora, a mirror, O

anything built round a void.
Jellyfish, puddle, vase, I recorded
meticulously, the currents, phases
of the Moon, the shape of a flowerstem,

an echo. Nothing I touched stayed
to speak. I understudied evasion, cracked
pots, sent out bottles and histories,
murmured over and over I, I, I ...

LIGHT-YEAR

Winter Solstice

there is a journey in the flabby mushroom pale
and rank smell of the woods the carmelite white
lichen mildew and the sweat of steam out of the deep
alchemic litter layers to origin of beech leaves

slowly you walk against the weather of the week
and no wren sings rocking in balance on a briar
no sunlight blaze marks bark pistachio green
weird on the boughs of one old apple tree

cocoons for fruit Egyptian cloth and bearded seeds
threaded upon the sky only through broken webs
look up to see a cloud pass as in clouded glass
nubs flailing on the air where no hawk rides or rook

all is in layer on layer an absolute of absence
tugging the heavy boots the roots the pull of loam
still sentient still the twitch of one fine needle
pointing you north and north against your will

Spring Equinox

where are the horsemen gone whose crescents here
held half the year to wane in water riding west
through sallow dustfall of the trees did they believe
the light had burrowed where a hazel bends

you who still walk the ash cast of these woods the flint
sparks to your ferrule or the gorse is tongued
see only ghost fire yellow green as accidie the catkins
brush on your sleeve the bird's metallic note

is it as lichen on a slate that Midas lingers
or is hermetic change the hidden heat
you stir iron sediment of pools incut in bark
the fingerholds of the December dark belief is over

beside the burnt out embers of a beech bole turning
you see the gleam you see the spent son of the sun returning
but what it is comes back to you from a remembered orient
is the cold color of the mustard weed whose seed is sharper

Summer Solstice

from fire to fire from seed to seed unmade
where twelve sheaves bleeding hardly makes up one
in distant meadows where the drum the frenzied reed
come into woods without a footfall heard

and is it sleep here keeps the birds so still
their nighttime noon green closes into green
tunnels of beech and rhododendron mines
sharp click of water burning dross of flies

not hum of summer or the fretwork sun to show
a breathing or your shadow on the ground
all intricacies pass the glass shows grass
clutching a lighted straw St John St John

search in that green vault where the bone went down
the pale drowned dogrose and the thorny briar
what hare to listen cringes in her form
what bends a stalk or quills the lovely fur

Autumn Equinox

beech trees are black after the rain the larvae keep
their mummery Anubis in the open knots each raindrop dark
of alembic catches the sulphurous sun seen only going through
the wood's long exit custom sets the balances you wait

until the bronze pan greens with verdigris one hedgerow holds
the barrowed bones of badger dragon wolf of Vortigern
Rowena's lips red beyond any sunset in the ripened fruit
of birds singing the thrush is quick the mole turns in his hole

fires into embers you take up a wand and climb
the warrens over Troy the warp of all things clings the weft
frays in the windless still to an idea of beaks remain
the first star says remain these are the lands I light

between one beech bough and another in this circle fix
your free feet on this hill until another turn and autumn equal
the harvest of the husks and in this match of light the light will marry
the line before your birth into the starline

SHADOWS OF LEAVES YOU CROSS

Shadows of leaves you cross our haunted summers—
Set in green caves beyond the slanting rain
The garden gods composed and mute as asia,
Hoarding the gardener's gifts, preside again
Over the garden's ruin and the barbarous years
Come under cover of those smiles remote and wise
Into the covert heart. Like swifts that skim
The level fall of lawns, their random spies
Report upon our walk, our gestures, talk,
Marking the just excuse to turn aside
That lets the arm escape the classic pose
Of love, of friendship. Boundaries too must hide
Unseen like ha-has. We protest the perfect view
Of gardens, white pavilions, cloudscape in the lake,
And trees that reinforce those long-drawn lines
Of choices trained to choose which path we take,
Formal, but dark with leaves, and ending at the gate.

"BIRDLESS"

I am told there is an island off Mexico—
in Spanish, The Island Without Birds—
no gull is seen, yet it is covered with guano.

I believe all travelers' tales tonight;
just as I believe in foghorns, earth tremors;
also in rumors of wars, old wives' tales.

Tomorrow the sea will be calm, the sky clear.
The island before us will blind us with white
droppings of absent birds; and the wonder of it
will be like one footprint or a single feather.

ARACHNE'S ISLAND

I think we have landed. I should like to think
the stones that grate under our feet
meant separate worlds she'd made for us. Hard, hard
the pebble on the instep, and the oarlock's screech
wrenches the dead web of the air
from our uncovered ears.
                              Fresh water,
only a drop, shocks something in the skin.
The sunlight scalds our eyes in each returning
from all the broken fragments, marble blocks
carved with acanthus or the cunic scribble,
like dung of long-dead birds, their beak and footmark.

Here all the pieces rest. Did we forget the puzzle
that worried us so long? Our memory limps;
our limbs made whole in more abundant water,
the iron roads of every distant morning.
Hard, hard to lose ourselves again for love of her,
casting her toils here over so much stone.

Look how the sea has fashioned these appalling faces
and driftwood hands that clutch for the soft spoil.
A drop of our blood would awake this island
into green murderous birth, a life too full to bear.
We are unready for such transformations,
our loss too little for a fearful change.
We long for fog to hide the sharpness of these headlands.
A sea too dazzling breaks and rolls its torsos
of gods and horses, tumbling over shingle.

I am forgetting why we came. Was it by moonlight
we saw this shore first over quiet seas?
What made us come? We knew the island barren—
how, even from far off, we recognized the dead
hulk of a waste the birds had long neglected.
Brush off the foul cocoons that stick like limpets
and walk towards the boats with wild returning joy.
While these white strands are frail take oars and break them.
Nothing too great restrains. Come, let us go.

ISLANDERS, INLANDERS

for John and Catherine Howett

Welcomed to islands over the long water
they jibe about our bow, inconstant kingdoms
rock bluffs, the sea mews, under spells of water
And afterwards in cottages with tiny gardens
remembered days at sea, the wind in wheatfields
runs tides up to our shores, our easy exile
ground on the pebbles, beached but always waiting

Far into continents, at night the freight trains
wail over prairies. Land by long extension
brings us no homestead. Out from glowing cities
on roads we count the poles, deep into darkness
place after place we touch no more than going

FROM A PERSONAL ALPHABET

A is for ...

Alas the apple
being in Eve's fingers
a grenade
and among Muses
both attribute
of merit
and of discord

who holding
such an orb
sees all Arabia
even to glint
of mica

and its ancient horsemen
riding loose reined
and murder minded
between a war plain
and the sun fired mountains

or
in another facet
polished to a pearl
or Flemish mirror
observes a girl's head
turned

her laughter also
spins the white rind
or red
precise
yet different

B is for ...

Making an almost invisible sap
of many things worth keeping
upon earth

creators also
of the most perfect shape
for building

masters of order
and economy

though what human being
would want a place
in their ideal cities

or to taste too often
the oppressive sweetness
of their product?

Yet, grown indolent
in summertime of thyme,
of lavender and clover

a need to hear them drone
under all other sounds
security like breathing.

C is for ...

Curled in a ball. A riddle.
Not a cat. This one unfolds
somewhat like feathers, or perhaps
like the peeled segments of an orange.
White, but yellow everywhere it meets
the green – almost gray green.
Painted by masters. Set by some
only against the snow.

E is for ...

The eye of the needle, eels, earthworms; also
the four blindfold philosophers
and the something in the midst of them
that is a good deal more than the sum
of their abstract enquiries and fumbling excursions,
many none too politely made, about him.

Growing impatient at last,
he has shockwaved off in search of some water,

an earthquake more than enough for a small province,
rendering homeless a gilliad or so creatures.

Three of the four philosophers he has crushed unwittingly.
The fourth, if crippled, sets off for a telegraph operator.
Nothing is too much trouble for science.
Alas, the wires to everywhere else are down.

Having dunged several miles of road,
the great beast comes to rest musing by a pool.
His infinitesimally small eyes are so sad
over their clinking drinks men grow melancholy;
he, if anyone, knows the date of his extinction.

K is for ...

He put on his scarlet robes
and all that gold
and went to the balcony

the people cheered and cheered
HURRAH   HURRAH

have I forgotten something
perhaps a head

without a head
there is no need of a face.

M is for ...

The multitude
fish out of counting
in seas turned
slate gray   blue   green

ants outnumbering men still
in one anthill in Africa

bats in a Texan cave

infinity on the fingers
an abacus
the hairs of the head

mere number
is its own beauty

an Arabian
turning the grains
of the desert
into the concept
of Zero

P is for ...

the purple of beans
the purple and brown
of tulip shells

things pulled apart
or simply laid on a table
to be stared at

No need to send for
Chardin or Heda
to pry off the second husk
we grow around things

A silence of sunlight
in the room
but also of stems

Better to leave the knife
on a plate
beside the oysters
already open
and the half-
peeled,
un-
peeling
lemon

Even the lemon
is not really yellow

it is disturbing
to call it yellow
or lemon

just as there is
another sense
assumed
in talking
about the purple
of beans

was in the parlor
not eating bread and honey
but looking at the rain on the windows
wondering if ever again
she could be a child in a garden
watching the maid hanging out the clothes.

A Jack, not of Hearts, paces back and forth;
his rubberized cape made slick by the rain,
he moves round the shining leaves of the bushes.

Ten blue bullets in his gun;
one for the white pullet and each of her chickens
who have been feeding far too long on bread and honey
while the ex-king was alive and in his counting-house.

He wonders whether his own children will starve
without him, the harvest rotting in fields
in a far province almost out of memory.

The blackbirds peck but find nothing.

R is for ...

the oldest symbol, so
faded and dusty it is worn only
by the very young

who dream about giving one
fresh from the garden
to each other

when literature has had
time enough back in the loam
to grow up as innocent
and senseless as they might be—

out of school, birdsnesting,
some unlikely and very
sentimental pastoral

the Golden Age
an age of roses
a singing again
of the green of Spring

Well, not to be coy,
here is one from my own time

without meaning
it is the loveliest of flowers.

S is for ...

Seahorses that are not horses
though they ride the tide
wrapping their tails around
thin streamers.

Something so intricate,
almost baroque, a joke
to think them in the sea,
a prince's toy.

Is that just size?
Imagine them a hundred times as big,
real nightmares then,
that armed transparency,
those atavistic eyes.

W is for ...

When the serpent slithered away
wormwood grew in the whorls
his going made on the dust.

The apple already tasted bitter:
clearly it had not been worth it.

Eve plucked the new plant,
crushed it between her fingers
and smelt it. This one seemed bitter too.
Why then was she quite pleased?

Something that was itself,
no shiny skin, sweet odor
of the apple;
no sinuous dancing either,
unsatisfying eloquence.

All lessons learned
from wormwood—
unpleasant weeds,
necessity of rust,
hints at corruption—
proved easier to accept,
gifts of another kind,
thieves' consolation.

Z is for ...

The horse with stripes of course
that will not be rendered
into basic English.

I shot two in Africa once
which is no great boast

they were beautiful and slow

watering with blue wildebeest
they make a perfect photograph

better than skinning them
in the heat, their entrails
like car radiators

to watch them drink for hours
nudging their stark reflections.

FIRST PRIMER

I am Adam.
She is Eve.
In a garden
We live.

This is Eden.
Eden is a garden.
Here there is a rose.
Day and night it grows.
Flowers do not fade.
Leaves do not turn.
Summer does not burn.
Winter is the shade.

While the grass is green
Lamb and lion feed.
Every fruit is full.
Every herb is sweet.
At their every need
They kneel down to eat.

High up in the sky
Hawk and heron fly.
In the waters deep
Trout and pickerel sleep.
All things that increase
Live in perfect peace.

I the Serpent am,
Enemy to Man.
In an apple tree
God created me.

MODIGLIANI

For E.A.M.

To trap the Sun
exploding suddenly
in fruit
on flesh—
the minute flame
crackling along the flank
of maize,
of woman,
torturing the gourd
in monster pain
or forcing pumpkins into summer.

To seize the Shape
with daring fingers,
subtle in surprise,
drawing the neck
like an anemic stem
out of the winter loam
toward that Sun.

To paint no landscape,
yet to paint
all people as the land
he knew
and still more human
than the rest could do.

THE COAT

God, what a fool to taunt him! I had come
through dark halls where my footfall made no sound
into a harsh-lit room with four tall tailors round,
one of whom held the coat high, on his fingertips
as though the cloth might flaw, held like a crown,
or loving-cup, offered from guest to guest,
but passed by other lips,
came to my place, four dark attendants by,
who took my own and dressed me in the coat.
'How well it fits!' they said.

I knew their interest spoke, yet it *did* fit, curiously. What shall I say?
I even found the musk familiar, found things too, the counterpart of mine,
coincidence, a key, a broken ring, a sprig of thyme—Did this mean more
than that our lives were closer than I knew? Yet I felt strange already, strange,
as though my key had turned, opened the well-locked door, that I'd gone in,
walked in his rooms, climbed half-remembered stairs,
found an expected desk, slid out one drawer—
yes, overlooked his letters, marked with a running nail each mention of my name,
wondered to see it there—heard a corrective cough—and turned ...

Thought, or thought's waking?
Something physical drew in
as though a stick
were twisted in the coat.

Trembling, yet reasoning still
that body-heat might shrink the cloth,
I, all the while,
watched where the twin lapels
lifted like claws against my chin,
felt wrestler's arms
take hold along my sides,
felt breath
stir through my hair,
felt clam against my shirt
that blood-wet skin.

Now for their help I cried,
yet marked each witness stand,
motionless, save their hands,
still fluttering,
miming, measuring me.
I turned and saw
that three-fold horror
struggling in the glass
as though to free itself
from some great weight of snakes,
saw it mouth silent screams,
return my stare
with stark and pain-mad eyes,
saw its own nails
claw from its substance
cloth with flesh and hair.
I saw it fall—
entered again
that rank and slippery place,
heard cursed and named the dead,
cried out I was betrayed,
grovelled upon the floor,
begged him return, claim, spare—

THE DICE

• •   •
              •
          •
            •

So this   It has been proved
is how   on the boulevards
you occupy   you cannot make plays
ivory space   without the one
each centered
assuredly   I mean
there   with only a pair

the ayes have it   one imperils
ambs aces
                                 without meaning to
or think   also upholds
of two figures
in a field   take one away
when each has   the two break up
a square of snow   without even
and each stands on it   a quarrel
like a tin soldier
                                 call one
otherwise   duenna
and elsewhere   rival
the sky merges
into the snow   any name
                                 will do
but we
isolate   it is
stand   the dot
on our own stand   O of drama
on our plinth
on the block   the singular third
top surface   a reserve
of our own   against silence
opaque box

nor could we meet
quite
if our shadows did

nor even be one
if the earth darkened

How they met
themselves
in a wood
in a pool
in a dream

and how

fearful

they drew back

"Not us!"

their feet
were already
touching

"Not us!"

No

only
in a wood
in a pool
in a dream

otherwise

only ourselves
for all time
only ourselves

I misunderstand
your meaning

meaning only
the spell
is cast wrong

or is this
the unluckiest
throw of all?

five, yes
but except
I balance myself out
I am odd, alone
with a tale
and no hearers

In this figure
the dance
truly begins

or say
the ways divide

one you claim
is ardent
and active

but the division
between the blocks
is arbitrary

one way
a weaving
through fire

as if thought
could not also be
fire

up then
on the ivory stairs

"Click click"
the tailor
says to himself
in his dreams

a leap
each time

your coat tails
coming on after you
like shears

yet your legs
stay neutral

They said lucky
who only stayed

not counted out
not huffed
or puffed

but the house
held

or aslant
stood
one elbow
on the wind

they said survived
who were only
still in

secure
secure
on the slippery
ivory

on the ice
by an inch

on the sea
by a plank

on the ledge
by a finger

in the game
by sevens

• • • •
• • • •

"I have moved
the earth"
says the warlord
"to build walls"

"There will be no
breaking of bones
within my armor"

the snow stretches
North and South
East and West

beautiful is the power
of the powerful

it has the whole world
in its spell

"Click" say the ivory teeth
"Click" says the trap in the snow
"Click" says the key in the lock

In the moonlight
I mistook the menhirs
for maidens

nine

or I thought
the meeting
fortuitous

or I thought
the cast fortunate

and when they moved
in dance
or seemed to move

coming or seeming to grow
towards me

white figures
with the shadow
behind each

I remained
there
where I was
drawing a line

as you had taught me
with the stick
you had given me

whether they stopped
first
or I fell asleep
first
I do not know

only I awoke
to find myself
covered with rime

and this child also
alive
and in my arms

This is the very pattern
of the dance

of groves
of constellations

who shall stand
at the center of the one
stands also
at the center
of the other

and must be whirled
twice
into an ecstasy
of all the senses

twice I say
not by proxy
and at the same time
for there is no mirror
no water or polished bronze
to make two sets
of the one dance

indivisible and
double center
either of swords
or wands

of arms
at last
of arms

This cast
is the diminishing
of the dance

fortunate division
seemingly so
the only one

as if the kings
static
in solemn ranks
watching the queens

were hopeful each
not one
owning himself
unpaired

or
as if a soldier
standing among the hosts
before a battle

seeing them wheel in line
as thick as snowflakes

should think

out of such numbers
how will I be noticed?

then let
the odd one out
after ordeal
or casting of the lots
be chosen
to lie in ivory vaults

or say these others
indifferent
cold
be black dots
in the snow

so I lie by her side
enfolded within limbs
not ivory only

so I live lucky in my bones
never so sure alone

Last of the casts
unlucky
too high
too heavy

no echo
of the dance

but hobnails
six in each heel
to print
the morning crust

"Clank clank" says iron

chained men
along the lane

freight cars in drifts
birds freezing
on the wires

the kings again
too sovereign weighed
to scamper into exile

all things immobile
locked in element
might massive masculine

ranked great in space
luckless abiding wrecks
left where they loom
passed with averted eye

JONAH

If Jonah never saw the sea or the whale,
If it was all a dream of Jonah;
If he imagined such a fear and shook
In his iron bed and sobbed and cried
And woke next morning, found his book
Lay open; in the yellow mirror, Jonah,
Thrown up; outside, the natural gale,
Blown out, branches across the lawn
And broken tiles, the shipwreck light of dawn
And farmyard squeals. He quickly dressed,
Shook only from the cold, yawned at his wife,
Finished his coffee and returned to life.

FAMILIARS

Mary's little lamb follows her
at the daylight gate
at the curfew hour

by the lane, by the briar
foxglove bells the wood
dead-nettles on the wicks
white mutes on a stump

what is it casts a light
so farrandly?

hawk on the barn door
flittermouse in the brown air
or the Crizum child
to the cross worlds nailed?

with stick and stake
with Mary's white lamb
with the hawk's claw
with Leird like a lion
with Tib and Tyffin
Fancy and Ball

at the daylight gate
at the come home hour

borne away with the bell
with water run backwards
the red bell flower

THE WHALE'S LAMENT FOR THE LOST WHALERS

Töten ist eine Gestalt unseres wandernden Trauerns …
— Rilke

KY reeeeeeeeeeeeeeeeeeeeeeeeeeeeeeeeee oh fara fara

The
white
fragments

whiter than
ice
less white than
birds
than

birds

falling

The
black
caul

Ky reeeeeeeeee Oh fara roah roah roah roah

knotted line
about
neck
or
ankle

roah Ky reeee Ky reeee   O h a O h a

Bubble
spinner

in firm green
in green waters

                    MY

                mate
                man
                mammal
Kyr kyr
        eeeeeeeeeeeeeeeeeeeeeeee eeee Oh Oh eeeeeeOh

            Caught
            caught
            caught

                hunt/
                    er

                kill/
                    er

        All the

            Waste
                of your wake

            the sing/
                    ers

                LOST

            the singers
                    lost

        trickster
        tripped
        trapped

                FALL/
                en

Kyreee   Oh   fara faaaaaaaarrrrraaaaaaaa
                The moon pan
                of my oil lights you
                white light
                lights you

fara   faraaaaaaaaaaaaaaaaaaaaaaaa

> with a white wick
> down the
> lost steps of your life

> LIGHTS
> > the singers
> > lost

> My torn bod/ y

> my grief as

> great as the deep

Ky   Reeeeeeeeeeeeeee Oh   fara   fara

> Let our prayer be
> let our
> prayer be
> adequate
> be spo/
> > ken
> at last
> let our
> prayer be
> > and
> > complete
> at the last
> be
> spok/
> > en
> together

KY   REEEEEEEEEEEEEEEEEEE
KY   REEEEEEEEEEEEEEEEE ORA ORA

> in the keeping
> in the keeping

> of the sea

LESSONS

I   Time

I think of the time from conception to birth as 90,000,000 years.

I think of the time from birth to one as 9,000,000 years.

I think of the time from one to nine as 90 years.

I think of the time from nine to ninety as 81 years.

II   Geography

I wanted to climb the mountain in Mexico
that was like a peony.

The Nile was thin as a thread
and so green.

Congo was a church bell,
deafening tone and drone.

O Orient!

Even I knew
Asia
was bread.

Pampas
wind in grass.

Irrawaddy
a maze of snakes

or was it worms
writhing
oozily in mud?

Chichen-Itza
the gnawing of small teeth.

Klondike
the clock
on the schoolroom wall.

Stamps
maps
globes

colors of
plasticine messes
girls' dresses
flowers in presses.

III   History

Q: What significant changes
   would have taken place
   if Abel had won?

IV   French

Monsieur of the dark coat,
you have cut yourself shaving again.
The children in the little square
are amused by chestnut trees.
And in the same garden of my aunt the gardener,
has he not eloped with Madame your wife?

V   Music

We will practice "The Ash Grove" for speechday,
but for going to the air-raid shelter we will sing "Run, Rabbit, Run."

VI   Latin

Following a number of unforeseen circumstances,
Caesar into winter quarters over the Alps
with all his cohorts and the hostages
he had taken in previous operations too
involved to be mentioned here
triumphantly marched.

VII   English

A lyric is one emotion sustained,
usually love or joy, but an elegy
is always sad and about death.

Poetry usually
rhymes, and must keep
time. I wanted to write an epic

about the war, but the soldiers I saw
were uncolorful, unhelmeted,
unhorsed; usually staring silently
out of trains.

Give me a subject, I said to myself:
I'm not in love or sad,
I have only the words,
English words, English names,
and the time of the rain,
and the false rhymes of schoolrooms,
the loose rattle of something
like window panes.

VIII   Maths

Multiplication by apples and pears
or by going up stairs.

Subtraction by confiscation
or coming down
taking two steps at a time.

Algebra by x and y.

Geometry by pie.

Division by groups and teams,
never supposed to be thinking or dreaming of myself
as just one
by any sum.

IX   Space

I think of space as the one place I was never in.
I think of love as the last thing to name.
I think of you as I think of myself.
I think of the children as I think of the children.
I think of death breath by breath.
I think of being alive too, breath by breath.
I think of beginning again and begin again.
I think of myself as I think of you.
I think of thinking which is only space.
I think of these words which are only words.
I think of our life which is only our life.

URBAN STREAMS

For Edward Thomas

Lullwater, Lapwater, Sweetwater.

I walk beside the banks of Brook Street
And wonder what it is that's underground,
Perhaps in sewers or in conduits;
What softened to the traffic long ago,
Under the wrangle of the trams,
The hansom's lighter grinding, trucks
That shudder, cars that stall and charge.

Coldwater, Clearwater, Fleet.

From tunnels, the pedestrians' feet
Would sound like falling leaves
From some long autumn.

Only the names are flowing above ground;
Only the sound,
Caught for a second in the ears like weirs,
Spreads a brief fan of spray, of foam,

On subterranean domes
Within ourselves
Casts their lost waterlights.

HOMAGE TO ST. NEOT AND HIS CHURCH

"Performing the usual unneccessary miracles,"
wrote an officious clergyman, C. of E., in the last century
about St. Neot, who had other fish to fry,
being an almost unknown Celtic saint
who could get fish literally to leap
out of the stewpond to a pan his servant held
when he lay sick, unable to angle for himself.
No mean accomplishment. Let the clergyman try.

All his legends in glass and Adam
who, dying, had the seeds
of the Tree of Life planted on his tongue
by one surviving son after the affair
of altars, so from Adam's corse
should come the True Cross. Other dubious wonders,
Noah, his chock-full ark, a Garden of Eden
with a most friendly clerical serpent.

One church that no iconoclast has plundered,
too far from whirlwind zeal, on a moor's edge
in absent-minded Cornwall, where a
necessary miracle preserves St. Neot's,
keeps the fish leaping, the seed
growing. And will, one piously might hope,
outlast all weathers, need for further comment.

PASTORAL

At the wood's edge we come on Caliban.
The boy's a roarer,
a drunken lout; wild strawberries
scattered like bloodspots near one hand. The other
clutches his member, center of gravity
in any man. He dreams of riot:
soft cuddled conies
bucking their back legs so,
does' quivering flanks,
the lambtails' frenzy,
all working into air,
soft, seeding, scenting air.

And that high brake of weeds
conceals the gaudy pards of Bacchus stealing
from higher lawns—
the ragged robin clashes with their gold.

It must be said
that this is Spring and everything is wrong
for patient pages. Even the birdsong jars:
"kill-kill!", "kill-kill!" is cried
about the grove. And cannibal as doves they come,
the local lovers, your Daphnis, your Aminta;
not coy the boys, not shy their country partners.

For this is Spring, a dream of Caliban,
not easy to be told. Bind up the scythe with flowers,
leave winter seas to batter round her tower.
Where Prospero's king how shall the brute world speak?
She reads all seasons one, remote Miranda.

PAST NEWFOUNDLAND

Tonight, watching the long ships glide
past Newfoundland—snakes with raised heads, how purposeful!
drive through the wastes of mist—I saw you,
thinking of Norway's mornings and the whinneying mares,
propped under waterfalls of white maned stallions.

At first you gazed through me, seeking a doorway
where the geese gather. Call my sometime sister,
a trout that thrashed once among trampled flowers,
leaving one element to die into another,
as humble as a basket, lost her random colors,
she bakes bread still for you who claim you claimed her
on the cliff meadows, sunlight, clouds and breezes.

Your earthwife's eyes grew elfin with foreboding.
Blue innocence, why should she shake like quakegrass?

How many years, the buried sun returning,
when you grew out of wonder with her power
to raise up bread each morning, or at evening,
after the black soup in red bowls,
from mysteries on yellow planks by yellow firelight
conjure one flame no wolfskin robes could smother?

She'll hug them to her now. And you imagine
she calls your name above the shrieking hail,
or storms that overhead like monstrous rockfalls
tip out of one high empty heaven on another.

No answer from the waste. Was it an omen
the gullcry at the crack of new found worlds
was pared to simple greed for no known creature?

Why should your earthwife open wide her dreams,
her limbs to hold you?
You've matched your fingers with my rings already.
My hair's your only tie. How cold a mixing
we've made of seas! Think of her grieving.

AUTUMN, ODYSSEUS

A window always open on the sea.

In the name of a name lost. The tide spreads,
enters coppery inlets; black out-thrust of rock,
twisted hawsers, windlass, and bristlecone pine.
A low shrub grows, the body hair of the old.

Hermit of the heart, to whom all rumors of
women are sirens, all silences rumor, you
with the greed of a gull, beachcomber of books,
who followed the seabirds here, tricked

by the other side of the island. A peacock
displays, eyelid and eye, mourns raucously
over its scaly feet. Out of the myrtle grove
rises the house, mother-of-pearl glow

on stones, unfamiliar becoming known.
"No!" you cry out. "No!
I rigged all this in a bottle.
Burned letters. Forgot." Down

sunglazed bluffs glides the hawk, over the
bluffs a shadow. Nothing is changed
for a name. A thorn clicks counting the coils
you climb in the dark stairwell.

Harsh is the voice that summons. She stirs up
dregs in a cup, her hair blurred red by the
light, her features. A dog at her feet
raises its head to greet you. Roses are rocks

as the sun drowns. Dark flows over the sill, over
the floor toward you. You see yourself as you saw
a young man enter the room, a woman bending to
roses, the sea and the window open.

IV

"Read Into This My Reading"

SIR JOHN BY STARLIGHT

Sir John by starlight sleeps deserted
Upon a table at an inn in England:
Within this belly now the stuff of battles
Slips from the white pikes and the rival armies
Rush into ambush.

                In this tun the hops and vineyards
Flow to their seas of amber and vermilion.
White ladies come to blush, to the bed's ending,
Their names remaidened here. From calumny
All seed returns into one fruit—the pomegranate.

A giant weight, a waste of memory
Lies on the board. Beneath the cover
Campfires are out, the suns in setting
Upon a hundred heaths, on foreign cities
Whose siege is on, who drop, soundless, to rubble
Under the ram, the rolling drums, the rain, the scuffle
Of rats' feet in the wainscot in this room.

Silent, by moonlight now, the shroud of snow equates
The winter plain, the lofty hummock,
The Roman features of this dead patrician:
Into a moth-mist now, into November,
The classic landscape and the golden stubble
Where the red fox lies slain, the wicked bluejays
Are hung on staves, their jargon stopped,
Their amorous, quick ways suspended

HAMLET

Nothing was rotten but the heir apparent.
We drank too much and gossiped, maybe; but the king
was vigorous, baited young Norway, kept the borders
strong, the court luxurious, and the relict queen
whinnying and lathered, very like to foal
by spring. Then the pale student came from Wittenberg
with ghosts of learning and an intellectual gift
for raising ghosts, giving raw bones a cause.

Half dead himself, he got up parts for death,
stalked spectrelike through Elsinore, trapped
dustmotes in his hands, and played at spies
with bumbledores and mayflies. Impotent with thought,
he lectured love and made a mad, wet nun
of poor Ophelia. The state drowned with her to the weeds.

Now Norway occupies us, and the court, what's left
of it, humdrums in mourning. Pray God for better days,
robust, unstudied leaders, honest Danes again:
wild drinking bouts, fair wenching, no more plays.

APRIL 23RD

Here on your birth and death day should I take a stick and stir
your basilisk of bones? If Stratford stones could speak. What,
gone, and left no blot behind? Your marrow stays the grist for every
scholar's mill. Where nothing's known, what comes of Nothing?—look around!
Where there's a will. If every pretty whore could sing

Cloves on her breath and cloven like the Queen, not crested.
Great rigged Eliza rides the Lapland Sea. The capon King
knights with a trembling hand the lenders of the land, gives you
a cuckoo's crest, rank if you live to wear it, widow's festering weeds.
News from reviews, the words are wrong in every skylark's song.

Not on your head that in the bogs your Irish poet peers
were slashed from ear to ear. Milleniums of lore leaked out of them
like sack. No hero met a Roman death that day. The rumor reached you,
if at all, out of some Falstaff's mouth—"to fill a pit"—to stall
a trencher with fat nightingales. Anon, anon, Dark Lady of the West.

Luck to your language. Every plot a jay. How with a little breath
you beat the bearpit's gate and had more true king's heads
than you could spend on stones, we know. Picklock is for careers.
Maggot breeds blowfly still. Your Globe is filled.
The rest's caesura, Prince ... lop-tongued Lavinia, Lucy's deer.

THE CASE

"Nay we measure the goodness of God from ourselves; We measure his Goodness, his Justice, his Wisdom, by something we call Just, Good, or Wise in ourselves; and, in so doing, we judge proportionately to the countryfellow in the play, who said if he were King, he would live like a Lord, and have peas and bacon every day, and a whip that cried Slash."
— Selden, *Table Talk*

Solemn arraignment in small letters
being the case of the mice against the cat Slash

They had a learned legal friend among the spiders
to catch large animals in a mesh of precedent

THAT their meat was necessary to themselves
and THAT it went best upon their own bones

THAT from the time of the Confessor at least
it had been recorded they ate corn and crumbs

The memory of no creature still living went otherwise
It was good Common Law and Ancient Custom

not to be set lightly aside for a cat's Statute
to creep in by tyranny and devour them

THAT they had a right to peace. THAT whatever pleased cats
was a crime that cried up to God for justice

MADRIGAL WITH AN ECHO

for Giles Farnaby   *and for John Berryman*

The curtain drawn, mists fly the morning   mourning
From grosgrained fields the heavy rooks retire   ire
A warbler, greengage green, lies all unruffled   fled
And long legged waders walk on pools of fire   fire

The curtain drawn, and all the world's awake   a wake
Blue crystal clears, frost strengthens its device   vice
In underwood, the raucous bluejays scold   cold
The tinkling stream plays organ pipes of ice   ice

If I have meant well, good to all I'd urge   dirge
Fortune or tune, what time and friendship mends   ends
All dark discords, past or the present error   terror
What distance lights, and what an hour suspends   spends

Construe my meaning, like a *toy* of glass   glass
I turned your winter's *dream*, all grief unguessed   guest
You sleeping by the green bird on white grass   grass
With all the cold frost burning in your breast   *rest*

LINES FOR QUEEN GERTRUDE

Drinking in Denmark is our *forté*,
not confession

Hamlet, you saw me in the garden
all afternoon with panier and clippers,
my face a trifle flushed, yet I cut cleanly:
each long stemmed rose
bled a green drop like sherry.

I was quite careful crossing lawns;
I never tottered
however tight my shoes.
I kept the pool in sight
but never went there.
The greenfly and the canker,
the snail seed on a stone
did not dismay me.

I could have faced the sly hair
under waterlillies,
the blowfly glutting in the rind
of vole or melon. You, I think,
are not a match for gardens,
or farmers' yards ... or women.

I should have told Ophelia
to make you happy is a simple thing,
to keep you talking,
closed to all present sense.
You are not rooted well,
you are not watered.

Lilies that fester, say ...
lilies that fester.
Or say that overripe
is there for seeding.
That must must have its place
such weeds as may be.

These knots and beds delight.
Look on it how you will,
my severed stock.
some things there are
too rank, too certain sweet
for thinking.

HORATIO'S SOLILOQUY

I am the figure that supports this stage.
Neither the midwife, nor the messenger
that brings life forth or puts it to the test,
I have a part aside. The action rides. I tend
to no apparent cause, nor, joining with the rest,
become a voice to rouse or mock this friend.

I am a man not bound by ties
that time or distance breaks. In each disguise
I know him for himself, though he goes mad and breaks
all rules of honor, love, or State,
and is deserted by them all.
                        I wait
upon his madness or uncommon pride. His fate
is mine, but mine without the glory, or, indeed,
that agony he keeps his own. I am his common need,
and when that passes, too, I pass from sight …

But know, beyond these boards, this accident of light,
I still am vowed (you whom the crowds disown).
Where one goes forth against the age
he shall not go alone.

KING LEAR POEM

It is old Caius who completes the play:
"I must not say no"—
After so many Nevers, Nothings, Noes:
"I must not say no."
It's Kent, as Caius, who completes the play.

It's Cornwall's servant who confounds the Duke:
"Better service have I never done you
"Than now to bid you hold."

Good masters may grow bad,
Kings and old men go mad—
He shows us when and how to disobey.
It is this servant who best serves us all.

It is the servant's No starts back the play;
Rebellion within love sets nature free.

It is Kent's "not say no" that makes a Yes
of great negation, vast futility.

LETTER TO THOMAS HARIOT

Aubrey and I were the first to discover you
some years ago one afternoon in the British Museum,
when I confess I was looking for Harington.
You came to meet us brushing your cuffs,
sneezing for bookdust in the fly-loud Bodleian ....
Or was it the London Library?—No matter,
the man who rattled Napier's Bones, invented
calculus before either Newton or Leibnitz
but didn't publish.

Ideas, you say, have legs. Keep them at home.
Starve them and beat them. Become another man's property?
Their great originals in any upstart's livery?

Were you then proud as Lucifer, your patron,
whose ten great poems escaped the printers' devils
to fall into abyss? Sound down in water—"Water!"—
The Ocean's Song to Cynthia, Eleventh Book brought up, a fragment.

Or was it that in Marlowe's ghost you feared a bishop?
Cerne Abbas, talk of Atheist and Machiavelli ...
One Walter Raleigh's man can conjure up a logarithm;
the comets call him Tom; his weird's a dormouse
quite like his patron's soul ... Hung, drawn, and quartered
out-Euclid's Euclid, geometry of living gut and tendon.

Small wonder you'd keep mum. A secret Papist, too?
A Parabole? Socinian? I forget what other.

Giordano Bruno's friend ... and Marlowe's ... and the Wizard Earl's!
Out of that midnight stable shall we find one pure? Hum, hum.

If you were put in prison simply on suspicion
(buzz Robert Parson, buzz, and Master Baines),
your health being broken so, need we look further?
In circumspection safe, safe circumspection.

Or was it that your papers just grew too confusing—
all those sly atoms whirling in the wind, what links between them?
A busy brain and no solution made to hold
what overflowed, those ideas in abundance.
—Come with a bushel basket by the door a'Monday.

The Reverend Torporley, named in the will to edit,
read on aghast. He gazed and floundered,
sent not a word of yours to print, but published
his own rebuttal to a work, by his neglect, not butted.

Bad luck in all things, then. Who needs executors?
We all do in the trade, or go as orphaned
as notebooks in a drawer for sabbath centuries.

You're known at last, but have a kind remembrance
of me, who found you first, admittedly with Aubrey—
one honest seeker, without grant yet eager
to help you from your grave. Now my green man's been stolen
by Resurrection Men without a claim to know you.

Well, there's a great book lost ... Let's on to dinner:
you, Bruno; Marlowe with Faust; Aubrey and I; Percy and Raleigh—
phantasmagoric food, urned nectar ... Tell me
what answers you found false, what true, silent in embryo.

LETTER TO GOETHE

Tapping out your Roman Odes on the shoulder
of a sleeping girl. But was that use quite fair?
All's fair in art. You say you learned
in love more than enough to save your idle hours;
studying would bring you less. And yet she slept.
You went on writing in your head.
You prospered did you? She
had dreams: Egmont? Faust?—or Pan,
Earth's older gods, danced to another drummer?

O earnest German wide awake in Rome,
making each minute pay. Love reimbursed your evenings
when libraries were closed. I'd fear to read you
beside my own quiet girl, whose dreams
alike elude me.
Where all's fair in love, she breathes
counter to counting fingers.

FOR WISE MEN

For wise men learning is the last illusion.
He sits and smiles among the morning trees,
A garden god openly worshipped by the nurses
Who tuck his rug about his knees.

His hands, spotted like leopards, lie in wait
To trap the tassels of his gown;
The books flutter in orchards where the wind
Has brought the branches down.

His wheelchair rules black lines across the lawn,
Thrushes crack snails against the gate;
In borders blurred with mist chrysanthemums
Like reading lamps burn late.

DIDO

If he's so weak he needs his Destiny
To make excuses when he means to go,
Or to invoke some subtle blasphemy:
That he's put on and blown thus to and fro
Upon Jove's errands, and his Goddess mother
Has bidden him to leave; but how he grieves—
You understand!—to do so ...

Am I to pity him his pitying me?
And this half-choice, this false necessity
That leaves me feeling ravished, never loved
By any man, now that he doffs that role
For hero, shade or godling (as he chooses)—
Even the dead have power Æneas looses,
Their breath was warm, though they walk other ways,
Robbed of their choice; the warm sea air returns
Each night; something of nothing stays
To warm my bed: while *you*, false guest!
Your absence dries like dew,
To leave me arched and chill, each dawn a death,
Each thought a loss, stolen by thieves who make
Dross out of all they seize, wealth into waste—
Who sow salt, ash and iron on the taste!

No curse follows you now although you creep
Double among the shadows to your berths ...
Stand up! You need not fear me, now,
Or after, in your sleep.
Cast off. Look on to Italy and go!
Dido has pride Æneas would not know.
A Queen will die to prove it so.

MEDEA AT COLONUS

Whether I killed my children or not is really
irrelevant. It depends which version you read.
Most women do, given the time. Certainly my
jealousy for Jason has been overrated, that
sailor! It was myself I wounded somewhere along
the long way and this rusts with an iron importance.
Ask the gods whether small sums make the interest.

It was myself. I had bitterness in with the dugs.
Only Cassandra might know … Most women, ah, ask me
of the common fate of women. What do they die of,
the good wives, long before pyres—small togaed men
walking like ants in the sunlight, their supreme self-
importance, after a trial, a battle, a race, or
wrapped in a golden fleece, whose hard day with the
Gorgon?—of childbirth, of bragging, of ice!

And I had the knowledge of drugs. A bitch, you
will say, for burning. But, no, that was later, that
was the last straw for some pennyweight witch. I
at least was a Sorceress. I commanded fear. Was there
any other way? I was asking for Love, love, but that
had not been invented. Has it been yet, Soror, sorrow-
ful Sister? Has it? Scratch the small blanket for warmth.

And the moon. Ask for it. Beg for it. No bull vaulting
will do, no cock fight, no squarebash with soldiers.
Save your raving, I've been to the slavemarket, too.
I've drunk dregs in the dregs, asked the way to the Orient;
I've drabbed it, ladied it, betweened it. And I'm cold, cold.
What offer then for the curse of Medea, the corpse of
Medea? What small thorn fire? What brand on the sea? What
royal road back to the sun, you lions, you lions, you dead lions?

GREAT AND SMALL

For giant Goliath it had always been enough
To stand in all his armor, beat his shield and shout:
"You milky puppies, why don't you come out
And bait your bear? I promise he's not rough.
He'll hug you to his heart. Come out you curs!"

When no one came he'd laugh, spit once, and stride
Back to the fawning women. He preferred
The smallest, kept short slaves besides,
And hunted with dwarf hounds for smaller prize.

Only his drinking cups, in fact, were of his size.
Even his sword was any man's, a dirk
In his huge hands. And yet he kept great rings
He never wore, amulets and sacred things
Locked up in iron-bound chests. He liked to work
His servants carting them about; enjoyed the sight
Of puny legs supporting mammoth weights; called them his flies.
And dressed them in his clothes like canopies.

So on for many years he shopped his fame
(He'd long forgotten they had any choice)
And all seemed set; until one day it came—
At first he thought it was an echo of his voice,
So unexpected was that brief reply: "I come!"—
To tell the truth the giant was at once outdone,
Though it detracts from David's victory not a mite,
Only God and Goliath knew he would not fight.

MOTTO

In the Týn Church in Prague
carved on a tomb is the best motto
a man could leave to others:
"Better to be than seem to be."

But, Tycho Brahe, you died
trying to keep up appearances
like the worst of us, among revellers
at the court of the Emperor Rudolph
who had ordered that no man leave the table.

Stargazer, sage, died beer stein in hand,
unable to rise, to risk the rage of a patron,
died of a burst bladder, an ugly death.

FISH COURSE

Was it a carp that frightened Theodoric?
Consider this poor trout with parboiled eye
Fastened on me, more vengeful than Symmachus.

What's your advice?
If you were hungry, too, Lucullus,
Would you risk dying on hooks or pass it by?

MUSÉE IMAGINAIRE

About temptation they were seldom right, the old masters,
Especially the Northern ones. What saint or anchorite worth his stigmata
Would have given way to so obvious a full-scale chimera circus?
And how was one supposed to react anyway to defecating half-monkeys
Half-melons, or cowhorned viragos with Spanish moss trailing from chin and labia?

No, the drollery is overplayed by Schoengauer, or Brueghel, or Bosch.
This is all for voyeurs. The saint in his cracked spectacles under a stuffed or
        stupified owl
Sees no evil, hears no evil, speaks no evil.
Perhaps he is secretly amused in a sly Humanist way. He is never in danger.

But when this clownish intrusion is over, some trial will surely begin?
Silent, in stealth, Italianate sunlight mellow as a mandorla or the brushed pile
In peach fuzz will slide over the hovel's lintle. A knife will gleam silver
By a litter of pure yellow lemon coils. The wanton wandering about of a mere breeze
May undo the concentration of hours, raising a few hairs of the saint's
Near bald pate, which is certainly not cloven by any blade,
Nor nailed to any gold plate, but very much alert to a housefly.

Nothing extraordinary in all this. The painter could hardly paint it.
Any professional would resist it. Nothing to cut through the husk
To the tight gray walnut of any man's brain, or bedazzle the eyes,
Or mumbo-jumbo the ears of saint, patron, painter, spectator—save when
In the rarest moment imaginable, riding beautiful natural birds
Seven times life size the unnaturally healthy bodies of marvellous sins ride
        gracefully in
Distracting every elder among us from prayer, shaking the half-heart to thunder
Under the stone bruised, plum colored skin.

LETTER TO MISTRESS ELEANOR GWYN

Dear Nell, sweet carrot quean, my marmalade,
Say that your exit was a mere charade.
Just as each night you ended Dryden's play,
Whoa-up the cortege bearing you away
To speak your epilogue, leap from the boys,
Wave your Grenada hat. Such equipoise
Would leave Death speechless. Brave encore!
Our Stage revive, our Royalty restore!

Save us from tippling and from masturbation.
You were the best spark of the English nation,
Who kept a sottish king half civilized
Through ups and downs till he apologized
For dying long, went out upon a pun,
Who'd ask your urging ever to have come.
"Don't let poor Nellie starve." One Cockney whore
'S worth Madagascar *and* a man-o-war.

Come back, my tangerine, my nectarine, come back!
The Court's gone Stoic. All for lack
Of Nell, a knell. The City's like a pyre.
They walled in Paul's after the Second Fire.
Soho's a ruin—crib, club, pit.
Our satire's farce; pornography's our wit.
Poor starvling art, the Muse's new striptease,
Milk blue and mumbling. Are these doped to please?

Or these paid twice, to watch, then write, these earnest men—
First punks, then sociologists, then punks again?
Even I'm preaching, Poll, my parakeet,
No canting hymns, no Anabaptist bleat—
Come back, we'd give you television time
To talk on drugs, on teenage sex, and crime ...
Oh la, oh tilly vally! Gentle Nell,
Is there a place beside you there in Hell?

POTIPHAR'S WIFE

Suffer in silence the boredom of the rich
that led to wars little and great
that overreached art for startling effects
that spiced the sauces and frenzied the labors of love

Siestas alone she thought of the sluggish Sud
the mud cake baking, the knot of exhausted snakes
The gnomen pointed to the purblind eye of the sky
only flesh failed a little like sand from a concave bank

Envy the slave who stank of the kitchen, or stank of the pit
who lived by the sting of a lash, who lived
in the secretive spell of rebellion, who gambled
a hand for a crust in the second the cook turned his back

Quickened with folly the flanks of a sphinx
Unpredictable monkeys chained by their loins and the Nile's
predictable rising and falling, accept to the end
the mischief of idle Zuleikas, the dogdays' itch of a god

HOMAGE TO CONSTANTINE CAVAFY

> *"He began to see the hollowness of a life devoted to sensuality, its fragmentation and its waste."*
> — *Poets in a Landscape:* Propertius

How would you feel, old master, about that one sentence
in Professor Highet's otherwise excellent book
I wonder? I do not share your predilection
for males. I understand how such things
could be. But I do not share it. However
your celebration of particular rooms in the past, your ironic defiance,
your feeling that lovemaking is the one thing
to get excited about—*Agitato ma non troppo*—forever,
that I share. Is it true for you, me, Propertius,
that we'll never outgrow what the skin hints is real? ...
Or be tricked after all by the schoolbooks and rulebooks,
our minds taken over by rote to be rid of good sense
after bidding indecent goodbye to the senses? ...
When we're old, cold, neglected, grow shrill
in our skins? That I doubt. There is Yeats to disprove it,
if we want another opinion. I prefer yours. It's quieter,
more confident, too. And your smile, old Attic admirer,
when they break me in flesh may suffice to remind me
there are memories yet as we grudge the last pass at Thermopylae.

BYRON AT MISSOLONGHI

The poet, exiled for unprincipled behavior, dies
for a principle, forced to the wall by rhetoric,
his own and other peoples'; needing a home,
chooses his nomad sack of canvas as he chooses
one of the indistinguishable bands
to be his friends, although he hates their speech,
having his own idea how certain words should sound
here in their homeland. Alas for Hellas!—
tied to demotic gloss and time's translation.

Death then, with medicines and browning lint,
how unromantic, smelly, if not unexpected.
The trick is where to die, and when, and which
of all ourselves to thrust into the act, first, last.
Dead of dead words, shards round chthonic cities,
of irony, of asking irony to pick up the slack ... and yet
it was not wrong to trust that Attic salt to work the rest,
exchanging death for Cause, firing a carrion pile
to light the helot night, to raise the ghosts of Greece.

STENDHAL'S MISS APPLEBY

Diminished in his memory to a sampler,
the tiny house where English manners sided
with every mouse against the fateful cat.

Slippers and furbelows. October sunlight
shone through blue windowpanes in basements
and climbed wisteria vines. Street where
the shaggiest horses dragged brewers' drays

that set off doorbells ringing with a chime
all down the rows, Westminster Road, toward
the river. Something still sounds, but duller,
a housemaid with a broom thumping a carpet.

How little left to write, despite of time.
The furious dance of threaded needles
colors in clocks, borders of ducks
so white behind the yellow bars of willows.

And you, Miss Appleby, whose very name
is green, lean on your parasol before that doll-
house of a house. Neat scalloped tiles
are smiles and tears, a semaphore of parting.

Your eyes under the straw made hazy days
of cornflowers, surrounded by a bloom
of plum, a bruise on your soft skin, a little
damp, anemia maybe, though such effects

no needlework can show, whose shadows
are only colored threads, whose cats have no
sharp claws, whose mice no squeaks.

RIMBAUD AT MARSEILLES

Nuns, figures of darkness so intense
That you eclipse the ward lamps' glare,
Though on your breast and crown you wear
The hard white cards of innocence,

Yet from the armory of your dress,
For all your vows, strange currents stream,
Intrude your womanhood into his dream
And turn his fever to one long caress.

So as you pass this bed, a face burnt black
By the Arabian day, your movement stirs
A boat a second time upon the Meuse
To lurch toward the far-off cataract;

And he's a child again, whole-limbed and half awake
Who sees pale poplars, tall as seraphim
Reel off, the rain clouds speeding in
To close the day; and all the dry reeds shake ...

E: You neutral swan upon that darkening sea,
    Turn to him now who cannot run,
    This poet tamed by time and sun,
    Calls on your name, Sister of Charity!

THE FIRES OF THE FATHERS

For my own father

*"Sooner than that multitude of slight sketches, blots, designs, etc.,
which my father valued so much ... should be scattered to the
winds, I burnt them, and so much more before we sailed, that the
fire lasted for days."*
                    — A. H. Palmer to F. L. Griggs, writing of the
                    events before he emigrated to Canada in 1910.

All Cornwall burned that Spring in gorse tongues
Yellow in the rain, when Samuel Palmer's son,
The ticket paid, waiting to sail from one world
To the next, at Sennen stoked the cottage stove
At midnight and at morning, day by day by day
With zodiacs of corn, the Visionary Vale
Where Ancients walked and talked—his father, Blake,
And Angels—by Shoreham churchyard, Beulah land

To save his father's reputation for the late,
The almost dull landscapes of Rome, of Wales.
The smoke blew out across the cliffwalls
To a grave Atlantic, went before them all
(Those moons of Shoreham) to the seagulls' bleak
And absolute erasing of the dream ... in fires,
In wind that seared the bone, the gristle of the eyes.
The seed was cast upon the unreturning wake

Of emigrants. While in the red grate walked
The fiery figures to defy a pious king,
Prophets and wild old men. Naked of all but flame,
They strode like Kentish wheat, a guinea gold
Against the yellow of the gorse, a dawn too red to look on long
And coals too fierce to rake. On Sennen's slate
The curse grows mild against those faithless, faithful sons
Who hid the Corn God from the jealous Sun.

REPORT FROM RHEIMS

> *I felt I was being stifled by the horrible stench that hit me as soon as I
> entered ... At the sound of my voice, which I tried to make soft and
> consoling, I saw a woman's head emerge from the dung; as it was
> barely raised, it presented the image of a severed head thrown onto the
> dung; all the rest of this wretched woman's body was sunk in excrement
> ... Lack of clothing had forced her to shelter from the stringencies of
> the weather in her dung.*
>   — Dr. Cottu, from a report on French prisons, 1820

Come out of winter sun, birdsong
brittle in the frost-flecked air, to read and reach
through darkness and stench to the thing
in the dungeon at Rheims, with the decent doctor
holding a cambric handkerchief to his mouth,
retching, afraid in the raw, rank air
of whatever might rise to answer, to claim
a share of himself, afraid of his own words,
the false tone, that summon a woman, naked,
sculptured out of her own dung, unfinished,
alive, afloat in that cloacal river.

Who comes to mind first—the doctor?—the woman?—
or that cathedral city, in whose fonds
flows the river, the daylight boring down
a stone stairway, a witness already writing
the report in his head in order to stay sane?

Why do I instinctively choose him, asking
what nightmares grew from the rot of archives,
followed his thoughts through professional years
to honors the city gave? He had nothing useful
to give you. Cased in the only cover you had
against ice, eyes, memory, you were proof.
His pity, our outrage rage in some other prison.

MANQUÉ

In fact, in fiction, in a dream Napoleon
wept over *The Sorrows of Young Werther*
while half his army drowned in the Berézina.

It is an imperial right to surrender
to the beck and call of authors.
How many suicides were there when Goethe
put his puppet to bed with Lotte's bullet
and walked away no sufferer from fame,
Sturm und drang abetted in one breast
the world not much worse, and Weimar
put on the map, that pocket Versailles?

Given a chance, we all like to weep
for something other than ourselves, and
better to read *Hamlet* than make a decision
about who dies and who goes home
after the theater. If someone else weeps
beside us while we are reading and because
we are reading, because we want our emotions
handled artfully, in the hands of an artist,
this sadly inartistic someone is only a distraction
that fails to distract from our chosen distraction.

We can, after all, pick up real life any time.
Heaven knows, it is always there. But a book
needs to go back on the shelf, to a library,
out of our hands ... To return to Napoleon, who was,
probably, no better or worse for Werther, only
a man who had tried to write one novel and failed
and moved on to other ambitions, to the drowning of armies;
and Goebbels the poet manqué, or Hitler the washed-up painter.

V

America, The Haunted Landscape

Part One: The Civil War
Part Two: Unfinished America
Part Three: Cabin Between Creeks

PART ONE

KENNESAW MOUNTAIN

At Kennesaw we piece together from pine needles
and undulating earth, old trenches, old positions,
guarding a clearing. Sunlight on the boughs
of chestnut, oak, blue pine, once walls of foam
that let the Israelites across, then closed
on the Egyptians. Did the Promised Ones
stay one day longer? Here was the Killing Ground
for clear-eyed farmers' boys. Tumult and forming blue,
misted by rain-soaked grass and wraiths of smoke,
still better targets than racoons or the quick squirrels
that never pressed to die in living lines
dressed by the right. A saber catching light. A brilliant rag
bobbing and dancing from the smoke on some wild errand,
twitched on by wires. It draws the firing up
into the sunlight. Hangs there for counted seconds. Falls.
And you are cheering out of dry mouths. Nothing looks changed,
but you are winning. The blue files stay, but these are dead.
The smoke is thinning. Birdsong returns. As now,
the woods seem still.

                You'd won. You held the line,
older, half starved, exhausted, but unbroken—
until the horseman comes to Kennesaw
to say you've been outflanked once more, that Sherman
swings South—ignores you—South, into your homeland.
And you must fill in what you held with dead and follow
to pick up what he leaves.

                We find your victory
more bitter than defeat, who keep our eyes alert,
watch other clearings; coughing through nights of rain,
Stand To for other mornings. We called you to a truce
this afternoon to succor what survived before your earthworks,
but no one came. It's six o'clock, the Forest Ranger
waits patient in his truck. He'll close these acres
after our settled dust with a long chain of links ...
Oh tell us what you saw. Nothing is won or lost
at Cheatham Hill, Kolb Farm, and Kennesaw.

ABOVE DALTON

where we were standing when the rain walked round us
with a jingle of mule tackle on the piney air
and a cat snicker of hog flesh twisting on a stick
like a live snake trying to get itself up
backing out of the fire
and a jug of buttermilk

brought by some girl so lean and piney herself
in her wet shreds of floursacks my heart hit me
not for love but the poor peakish look of her
and for bringing up buttermilk

coming up that mountain in the snarl of a spring morning
to a camp of men who were no better than you'd guess us
and setting the jug down on a stone like we'd ordered it
and going off without a smile or a word down the path she'd come up

above Dalton one day in the war when the rain walked round us

CHICKAMAUGA

for Bell Wiley

white lightning on black water of the swamp magnesium flares
pitch on their bodies and the giddy licks as fire
comes up the creeks catching at bushes crumpled heaps
of clothes that rise up rigid then slump back
into the ashes as the fire pours on
over the water over the lines of men

give me a rope of vine to grope at give me more water
give me a way to reach you through my pain

across the tranquil acid slopped in Brady's tray out of
the sepia prints hung up like skins to dry

to scream in the mosquitoes' wail or burn aglow
in fireflies crossing now the wastes you know
cool lids of twilight Chickamauga's risen trees

SHILOH

the lot of the fathers all remember the rain and the broken chapel
at Shiloh tabernacle of the ancients and the yellow wounds of
so many pines there were more men felled than trees but it was
the trees that bled yellow in Miller's mind for ten years after
the event now Miller is trying to unbuckle his belt to let the
swelling inside make a Punchinello out of him four men face him
sitting as though round a campfire and each one has the same
exactly the same bullet wound in the forehead almost without
blood it is papers not blood they have turned out their pockets
of playing cards letters string old newspapers desecration of groves
when the kings came to Shiloh when Esau saw the gray pottage of the
young men scattered he wept the inheritance was Jacob's he slept in
Bethel seeing the angels climb a ladder of wounded trees he was
mortified with the rememberance of what his landgain had led to he was
exiled in his own heart and the land that was his now was nothing
it was an abomination he was rich in the hatred of dead men the ark
was lifted out of the mud and sand and carried to Pittsburg Landing
where Grant the dark lion sucked at a dead cigar and moaned like
Saul in madness I brought you back into Egypt Cairo and Memphis
to fester away the pines are as yellow as Custer's hair they are
running resin like rivers of honey they are the lights of groves
they lead men into union a united states of the night the
surgeons' lanterns are beautiful in the tents as sulphur
butterflies the limbs of Rameses are laid at their door
they struggle in mud but are separate who has sunk under here
who has lost the meadow out of his eyes as the wagons unburden
or the patient horses black mud to their eyes are bearing away
the ground stampers the builders of cities it is a Beelzebub
of flies we have established here east of Eden the chaplains
and looters are abroad in the land they spy out gold mice
among garments rolled in blood one touches Miller who pretends to
be dead as hands take out a Bible from under his shirt remove the
ten dollar bill let the Bible drop into his lap crawl away to
the paper searching through it taking nothing there is nothing
to take may the ten dollars stolen turn him to salt may shame
make a beast of him howling repetance at stones this is the
pay of the day species got with the milling of men it is not good
in the eyes of God it is no longer a marker in His book He bears not
with conceits of the braggard He will deal in the dark with the
wrongdoer it is well away what was earned for this harvest His pages
stain with my blood did I not know His signs that I sinned
was I an innocent that I went with the daughters of Lilith

and made with the strangers of cities this second covenant to be a
worker of wrath do Thou God with me as Thou willest he is eased up
cursing against further trespass carried off on a cart to the Landing
how did I come to this place he asks an old man with a knife
was I better than they who lie out in the rain was I chosen

SOURWOOD MOUNTAIN SONG

like a saw snagged in wood
ten years and every word she said
the whine and the clasp of grain

a line of Byron and an old song
about Miss Mousie and the courting frog
and the war came and I was roving
and the teeth stopped in the log

then the silence was like a knot
even when bullets snapped trees
I was listening always listening
and the killing went on over my head
like the tune of a liquored up fiddler
and the boards bucked under the dancers' feet

and I went roving in the moon
the woodsman's moon and the soldier's
and ached for the listening and thought
of the bullfrog courting and Miss Mousie
and the small white teeth of the saw

and nothing of this I shook off
till I came to Sourwood Mountain in the Spring
and hung up my gun and drank cold creek water
and saw the leaf claws on a rock like a bear's
and the gold sand in the bottom of the stream

and made up a song to go with the circle
I'd walked any weather and under the moon
how the fiddler'd be sawing there still
and how sourwood made the sweetest honey

GAINES MILL

read into this my reading I was the shade page of
Hector that hour in a gloom of trees and have
intervening
surrendered nothing not the sting of an
insect nor the odor of the guns

though Achilles cried out from the trench yet the
bells of Troy were nearer behind me it was the
last light of the day I was sixteen that summer alone
and how many were with me

there were apples there. Now some say there were no
apples in the pit of the valley but I say I saw
apples and smelt them and the mash of them under
men's feet in the hurrying

and I was amazed equally by blood and the way
the ground sucked up the essence of men it was
greedily it was hog like and black lipped
and I was afraid to be drained
from the soles of my boots
in the shallows

and I thought of you in the time of the splintering of trees
and my bones aching not to be snapped I remembered you

drawing your skirts up a little to be out of the dust
as you walked down the road away from me
going home I suppose in the cool of the dusk
I remembered you

not that your name was Helen who had laughed at the book
and the fancy of it
nor would you see me nor know that your name was my armor

not for the shaming of you Andromache nor for causes
except that that city should stand for my Troy
I was shamelessly neutral

but say your name now is it lost let it linger a little
and I buoyant in blood and unkillable

crash through the mass of the Greeks
oh the terrible Myrmidons

hack for the ridge in my rage in the tumult the crackling
of underbrush buffet of bodies the hewing
breaking like fence posts before me
the waste of their faces
press through their lives
the hot charge of their breath
and the chime of their buttons

but for you I survived on that night is it easy
to see near that house on the brow of the hill we had taken
in my jacket of blood I am photographed still
by the glare of the Argives' bright boats

it's for you I am smiling

SENTRY

when the squirrels tobogganed down the tiles in
darkness over our heads and the wind knocked out
its pipe against the panes like father on the
hob of the fire and the boards of the old house
about us stretched until I thought the nails
would be popped out of their holes like bullets

brother we shivered under the quilt our insides
sloppy and aching we counted off a third breathing
thing in the room and made massacres of the fire
tiptoeing under us where our scalped parents slept

later years we each slipped over windowsills to be off
in the night in the same or in different directions
crossing borders in darkness at the same call of wars

and now my brass buttons taint with their ominous
smell the chill air before dawn and click like a
catch drawn or a fingered bullet when I brush on
the split rail I stand at to watch in the woods
the eight shades of black exchange edges

what animal walkers or birds stalk over my
shrilling skin and what dry leaf scrapes
its razor block and wanders metallic under
my chin what rat mixes its hair with my hair

while you visit me either alive or dead for the
letter's late which army you never said yet
you near me and what fearful whispered tale
do we dare tell across dark against fear

pass kinsman
by blood only neither by left side nor right

MOUNTAIN LAUREL

what happens with the weather and no more
to cut a bough and whittle rings for weddings
and whistle up good luck and go to war

and what I had to tell was not worth telling
how I kept half the flowers in my head
and she had turning trees I never saw

while she went walking with Lord Randal or some other
I had a second and more constant lover
what promises I broke I never said

those songs she sang I never heard in prison
what happens in the high winds happened there
men were by morning who by night were dead

I turned the ring and wriggled out of winter
and now I'd sooner ask a favor of the rain
than ask the old buds on the boughs again

pale mountain laurel after any July gale
whatever wind I'd whistled up I found
some blossom's just as pretty on the ground

MALVERN HILL

for Jean Farley

late summer sun drawing the swastikas or sundisks of the wheels
in shadow wide across the wheat from guns
and the crows' clamor swallows skimming stalks
of guinea gold
on the plateau the river's loop a scimitar of steel
or section of another greater gun wheel
and in each quarter massed quieter than clumps of men
the quiet trees

below the slope debris of broken charges blows the poppy red
blue ribband band white stars of banners and in a corner
of a split rail fence holding against his chest the staff of
one such battle flag sits Clayton as if thrown
into that angle by main force

black powder tobacco oozings flies
ferment about his mouth his hat like a squashed piecrust
under one hand still flopping fluttering
as frantic as a bird
some pinioned fledgling
involuntary quick
tries to escape the nerve's dead center
in the man

Listen to me you angels
perusing avenues
strands of white sand and oyster shells
under live oaks and moss

Listen to me you angels island ghosts
the white robed spooks of slaves

Listen to me you angels come at last
over scrubbed Sunday benches over piers
where the white bobbing rowboats ride
blue Carolina bays

Listen to me you white birds of the swamp
or the brown pelican flotillas
of the sea

Come to me now come gather up the bread
in broken picnic bits spectres of peace
long promised peace
come with your baskets
dressed for the markets on the mainland
come

CHIMBORAZO

Chimborazo Hospital, Richmond, 1862

On Chimborazo, Richmond's canvassed plain, say that I walk
more than the wards—whose feet make no peaks in the bed—
move through the sulfurous air and clouds of floating lint,
to stalk a bandaged sky, swing upon starry lamps, or spread
great sheets, cool caterpillar tents, over those lying far
beneath me on the larval floor, poor fluttering wingless
things, scorched there by their own eyes, automatas who wave
bound limbs to pluck the sting out of the blowflies' whine.

Say that I walk before them like an insect god. Christ walks
on Galilee. The locust walks the wind. The mantis, holly twigs.
The whirligig walks water. I climb rungs of fire, or rise up
with a wheel, whose fans blow on their remnants, rally living
back, until they turn cold gold below me, crack their yellow
mask, and smile—as if bird-priests had touched their veins
with magic blades of jasper, freed the lacquered earth, the
armored heart, spun jaguar calendars back to mists of origin.

De Leon's lure lost in gray cypress swamps and live oaks
wound with mummy cloth, black mud, and orange water. Say that
even here, like some white egret, heron, insect-bird, I rise
into the higher air. I circle, circle slowly, float, the ghost
of every shadow's hope, each burning atom's opposite in ice,
pain's poppy dust, hell's heaven, thirst's water, drowning's
land, youth's age and age's youth, whatever's not ... my limbs
on Malvern Hill, my gangrene dream sleep walking and awake.

PEGGY LEE DOUGLAS AT THE DULCIMER

What cavalier at Nasby dead
Had a coat turned
By a farmer's daughter?
What brine has dyed
The white silk green
As it floated over the water?

So fond a favor and so flawed
With a heart of cross stitch
Half unlucky
And a doeskin band
Tacked round the edge
As it came to west Kentucky.

No sulphur rose
In the dark brake grows
So fair as your hair, Mat Allen;
And no dress could wrest
The cold from my breast
When the owls call down the valley.

COLD HARBOR

I have died three times already here where dog eats dog in the
Wilderness anticipate anything a fourth death or simply a
change beyond recognition the rain leaks into the marrow
bones of a man it exposes the running gutters the luce of his
being my scars are no longer the exaggerations of a spy you may
believe what you hear what the wind says in dried cornstalks
in a winter field where you are the chill of wet stones or
the wind again on the teeth of a man running open-mouthed
over brown plains of buffalo grass where there is nothing
to stop the wind on the morning before snow falls here we also
have cut such a swathe through the woods in order to see
gray ghosts of men appear at bone heaps of fences to bore
more holes in an old rag to worry a wolf from his lair
in the urinous earth there is a stink in my moving now
no undoing can mend I am earth flayed to origin the fleas
go elsewhere the crab lice leave me the sap of my man
fat is expended I have buried your letters in damp leaves
like a dog his bone I shall not return there is no reality
in such things or there is as much reality in the bag
of a groundhog caught in the fork of a tree I have survived
myself three times how shall I extract myself again out of
the earth no I say no to myself I have come after all
home among roots it is just as I expected even when I was
with you earth gun metal coffee grounds and the musk of men are
one odor or the eye gristle is only the bleb of ice on a stump what
glitters is ice or mica or gristle or metal you'd be bound to
mistake what has never shone in the dark even my bloodstream slows
to the pace of any underground river I no longer can tell
my hands from the bark or the back of a leaf this is the
husk and the shard I have chosen to speak to you out of a
pit picked clean by the winds I found sanctuary here
I am free of your voices be calm I have outrun your love
I have won beyond echoes this end in the quiet of my skull

ROPEBURN

Kennesaw Mountain, June 1864

spent to the broken soles of his boots
he lies on his fakir's bed
of snap twigs and twisted root
watching the spiders
builders on the wind
between boughs of the flame azalea

what blossoms on the blue sky
and the spider silk running off
quick surges of sunbeam
in a giddy rhythm
light flying as waterlights

the rhythm of his breath coming hard
under his open buttoned shirt
and his fingers cracked and burning
and his wrists red raw burning
and his back racked

getting the guns up Kennesaw
winching and wrenching and tug of warring
the terrible Napoleons
slow wheeled up rock and root incline
a man could hardly walk up
shedding rifle and pack
to stand on the summit
and spit down on the flat
of invaded Georgia

getting the muscle breakers
the shin crackers
the root draggers
the treacherous roll backers
up Kennesaw
to stand aloof in a cloud
and toss curses of Jove
on blue ants on the flat
of the meadows of Georgia

and what ice cold orange blossoms
what wet spinning spiders
in a dog day of summer

what quick climbers of light
what cool crumpled flowers

and him almost crying from ropeburn
thinking again of his girl cousin's voice
"does this hurt"
and her hands
twisting this way and that
in their long resolved tussle

MIRABELLE

what the avenue led to
only a child's rocking horse rocking
on the lawn and two diamond studs
at my feet just the right
distance between them
to be a man's eyes
or a woman's
shining up
each with a glimmer of orange
out of brown laurel leaves
and a patch
of odorous black mud

the noon hour
so oppressive in sunlight
it set the faces of stopped clocks
everywhere
in tree limbs
and the same cracked pattern
timed tributaries
split second stations
of spiderwork
in walls

only the cicadas
were winding up time
with a wheezing
of rusty springs
of ratchets
of keyways
and wheels

winding up what was dead here
dead as a photograph
of all of us
the fire and the diamond studs
nobody stooped for
and the horses waiting
as if carved out of wood
and only the wooden horse
rocking

and the gray
gauze trails of moss
animate on the wind
none of us felt
swaying over the house
that was going
under our gaze
in a sleepwalk of flame

DRIVING THROUGH BUTTERFLIES IN KENTUCKY

Black wings zig-zag before me, open this back road,
where heat eclipses the sunflowers, where I am the only

August dustraiser, disturber in an hour trumpetvines
close. Water moves between boulders as if uncertain

how to go. The speedometer settles on fifty. I plunge
into tunnels of walnut and oak. And now light wings

cling, are clamped to the glass, brighter yellow by far
than tobacco leaves in the bottoms. Half-an-hour,

we ride on together, flee East past Springfield,
leave behind us the packed dead of Perryville—

those gray stones riddled with sunlight and lichen,
four hundred huddled under the trap door ... O angel

in the light slanting between cedars, hold back
the green tide breaking! And the wings break up

before me and go floating, increase of swallowtails,
out across cornfields, the long shadows of Shakertown.

NOTES TOWARD A HISTORY OF KENTUCKY

I. Burying the Dead for Braxton Bragg (Perryville, 1862)

October has opened all surfaces. Even the earth
in the wagon shade grows cobwebs of cracks. Our sweat
spits back at us like bacon grease from a skillet, and the pit
takes on more yellow rows like cornhusks. Tell me
the blowflies' invasion has crested. Untitled stones
look Southward, and white letters of dried grass
wave to the brave going under a fieldhand's spade.

The general lolls on his horse, cursing his luck
all the long dusty road from Kentucky, leaves the nameless
to dig their own graves, his conscience crazy as bobwhites.

II. Morgan's Men Entertained at Pleasant Hill

Bring out the fresh baked bread for the world's raider
Who left Shaker horse in stall and the barns unburnt.

Bring white linen and balm for the battle trampled,
The boy black with powder, the stricken stranger.

Make a feast for Morgan with butter and apples;
For the men of war in the peaceful meadows.

III. Cistercians Building in the Year 1862

If they would speak at all, it would be in Flemish,
or some gutteral Franco-German, saying "*Allons!*"
"*Zutritt Verboten!*"—translated to the world as "get lost!"
They build a fortress out of handmade brick like Vauban's
to shelter silence in, flying the old French *fleur de lis*,
while all around them, farm boys moil each other into
carrion under their stars, stripes, bars, their banners
leaking out blood like baskets from the guillotine. *Pax!*
God's not mocked by these Napoleons, shaking the glass.
The smoke from Perryville gets in the choirmonks' lungs
at Compline. Flies multiply in windfalls. Crows desert
from sycamores and cedars, fly to the chattering guns.
That music's not Gregorian. Your prayers, perhaps,
snatch some souls, fathers, from the grape. Brick
upon brick, gray faked to look like stone. *Allons!*
Peace, perfect peace. Neither to save or strike the Union.

FORT BLAKELY

April 12, 1865
From The Merriam Poems

*Henry Clay Merriam is the white colonel of United States
Colored Infantry. He has just won the Congressional Medal of
Honor for voluntarily leading the final charge of the Civil War,
April 9, 1865, Battle of Mobile.*

Frogsong replaces gunfire,
hardly less strident in the Alabama night.
I wake a hero, leading the very last assault,
a name in Washington. The uproar is so strong
it carries the fields skywards
under dim stars—and peace
must be a matter of degree, and hard to learn.

Here, four years South of Maine,
I think of Lucy Getchell—then of men
missing at Pillow and Port Hudson, while a weak
Gulf wind tries hard to fill a flag.
I catch myself at times drifting like sedge
on some Sargasso of the frogs;
the pulse of distant breakers reached for, missed.

Six thousand prisoners captured, men
so desperate tired, so mean, so potashed-skinned,
they might have been short trees
that stepped out from the swamp. My own,
anxious; already seeing a trick—not mine—
rigged up to mock their victory. This year
no Jubilee, only Fort Blakely or the Crater.

Sergeants grow cynical. I said to them:
"I've done about all I can do. Promotion's
finished now." "Like pay," one whispered;
"Freedom to starve in Peace." Two words
I felt that I was rich enough to give away
like nickels once—at least in my imagination.
This is a lie I know when to surrender.

Dawn and the terrible Spring sun. The wind
is on the track of every kind of carrion,
bloated, half-buried dead, whose shirts
no longer button. I'm going home to marry.
I'm twenty-seven. Thank God my body's sound,
unlike my brother's. Oh, mention it in Portland—
I'm here, at one end of a war, with all my life left over.

DRIVING THROUGH THE WILDERNESS, NORTH VIRGINIA, IN A BLIZZARD TO RACHMANINOV

Strange in a maze of trees to find desert horizons, places
where once I wrestled to be born pure sense, uncommon master
by touch, taste, smell, hearing, sight, over the re-play mind.
I read the signs. It is a battlefield—three battlefields—and all
the hazard is in trees, the blindfold of the snow, and speed
that flicks the trunks like spokes, become a test to be. 'We warred,'
wrote one at Spotsylvania, 'against a forest', and for all their guns
the forest won. The wounded burned in leaves. The dead were hung
like Indian dead in baskets, root and bough. Trees buried them, regrew
as neither army did. Grant blundered, bled out Lee, blundered, forced
victory to Pyrrhic – half an army to regain McClellan's lines. What strategy?
Might makes the difference, spend it how you will? Widow the land, but win?
Burn Richmond, let jackals in in Washington, die cancerous, conscience-mad
writing your life, failures too vast for words? Grant us a death
less horrible—caught on two claws, stomach and memory—scraping at nerve.
Ride out the notes of Ashkenazy: dusk, forest, snowfall, dead—odor of
ice, earth, leaves—embrace of loneliness, waste of all civil wars
without, within. Keep sane. Keep small the crimes. Snow softens
nothing. In a gloom of trees the North Carolinians shoot down
victorious Jackson. No irony outflanks the hour, these ambuscades.

PART TWO

UNFINISHED AMERICA

unfinished america the raw orange pelt of the beaver and the road
giving out in the clay between ghost gray cotton bushes somewhere
in south georgia and the mountains the axel and heart breaking rock

heights where abraham somebody sacrificed isaac his last this third
day of september eighteen-fifty-one to the god of endurance and had
no strength left to bury his son but gave him to the birds of the air

and the apple brown woman born county clare by the door of her sod house in
somewhere nebraska maybe giving a look to the land all around her that would
flay a man down to an animal scream knowing his debts had all come home and no

seed left to plant for the next season or even in the calvinist cold
burial lots of new england unsettled settled the restless anger with
god and with england and the huckster and preacher rasping and whittling

the conscience barebone frenzied with unfinished business and even henry
david thoreau's enterprise lock stock and barrel declared bankrupt on two
cents a day and his beanrows going back to the wilderness and only the lilac

lovely luxurious sweet scented seeming to mock at the stonepicker stone
breaker stone carver stone farmer paying his way in the panic of this year
or that and the fish bones shoring up credit and the lifers making a new

contract to be quit of their god-debts by fall at the latest and move on
move anywhere to the beautiful barrens the mocking bird singing and the
gophers loafing and the passenger pigeons darkening the sky by day and

unfinished america ...

FAR FLORIDAS

Night moving and the fixed full moon
over the swamplands where birds' voices start
the rumor of great journeys

Frogs are the shipwrights of the shipwrecked earth
Methuselahs before De Leon came
old bearded man
looking for moving water

Live logs propel themselves
in the Ur-Eden
vast ripples black and white

The cypress stains and stains

A quiet of clouds

No going from here
What the intruder seeks
beyond far Floridas

No flower uncabled
Bearded with weed
the fleet is anchored here

Put out the flares
Ambiguous sirens never lied
They too were old

Whatever fountain sought   he finds
His youth unguessed at   Night and paradise

NORTH WEST PASSAGING

I see the crossing of light on two stalks
the bone china clicks together in the cupboard
the old woman draws closer to the fire the
palest of flames Montana and the morning
and a horse running off something stronger
than the gad of a fly in a far meadow some
wildness other than the youth and the beast
fever in its blood a madness of being maybe a
thing to fear watching and watching for the
slow movement of red clouds and the shadows
of peaks here the river brought us and now
pushes us out into eddy water into the slack of
motion an eerie suspension of the former
drive and the rocker rocks and rocks the
china in the cupboard at the edge of things
like a ripple running out but unlike the
hoofbeat of the young horse with the frenzy
of itself running through the roots of the grass
to the steps and the boards under my feet

To have come so far driven by the force of
I say the river something like a river
a river in flood carrying all this and
the two of us to shore everything under the
impassable peaks in this place of meadows
where what carried us suddenly slackened or
nudged us like an animate thing to the side of
the uprights of a bridge the bone china and
the cupboard the rocker and a mess of dresses

And the horse still running and the rocker
still rocking and the sun hardening on the
grass and the clouds still passing changing
their colors very slowly the beat of the
hooves driven out of my legs resisting
the undertow easily the faint pull back
into the frenzied gait of the colt and
the old woman trying to make heat from
the flames and the flames paler
frailer than sunlight to have come so
far only to watch and rock and have missed

whatever it was without even sensing
the moment it happened and knowing
only the miss of it now and the beat
going down into roots of the grass
and the mountains reversed and the
river and light and the heat
outside us and passing
between them

IBO

Were never slaves
the Ibo tribesmen who
at St Simon's Island Georgia
seventeen something
walked straight off
the slave ship
into deep water

one for all
all for one

chanting
swinging their chains

and were never recovered

OHIO WINDOW

It is eight below zero, the foal
his coloring elusively yellow
as willows in winter, clouds air
like a brook under willows, yet sets
each hoofprint in snow like the first
black stroke of a lettered creation
so is Alpha, is Aleph, Beginning
Cabbalah of language and cold

And I behind windows in warmth
a meadow away and a road—
if I think that road still into snow
which has fallen all night as I slept
and leans from me in morning unmarked
as the fresh sheet of paper I take—

at the table spend time without thought
watch the horse, fingers resting   then strike
those black tracks back to somewhere to start

LAS MILPAS, NEW MEXICO

It is summer, but these foreign hills
are green as almonds, the museum keeper's garden
up to its walls in weeds. A sometime fountain,
dragged half the world away from Italy,
is choked with cottonwood.
                              I have transplanted
such European thoughts, who watch the children
in red shirts on dark ponies riding
through clumps of goldenrod and sunflowers swaying;
have seen the hills a moment past as Sienese, as a Sassetta.

At least the birds will suffer no such imitation:
not Paolo and Francesca, not Ugolino—
names in a book the sunlight warps like the arroyos.

We cart about our great trunks, our intentions,
against mere wandering. Came Coronado
cased in his Spanish armor, dreaming of Cibolas,
and found instead of gold the pale adobe,
still better here than bricks for building houses.

TAOS PUEBLO

The rectangles rise up against
the soaring triangles behind
and have these twice three hundred years,
man-made, yet held there by the drum.
Man builds in clay and straw, the gods
mould man in clay and straw, the drum
speaks to the gods, the gods reply—
Hands hold the house and hold the man
and hold the mountain in the sky
against the wind that blows the straw
and blows the dust along the ground.

NOT SEEING FOR LOOKING

Coming back to the chicken jerks of a fiddler
sweat like plumjuice on my shirt, and the air
almost burnt out in August, boots peddling down
dust for the tune, old women, their faces like
flour sacks, showing faint letters through

I lean on the hot metal of the blue pickup
and watch spirits dance while my gas tank
is filled. Minutes I ride the notes. Not
to be born into this, or have played in wrecks
among kudzu, but something I yearn for, turning

my car toward any mountains I see south
of the Ohio—going home, who grew up on
boats, trains, the Atlantic, which was no
bad thing to form on and forget, so that now
I can pick any tune I like and miss it

even while I'm hearing it, tap my boots
kick the long pods of the locust, set wondering
if even the South has enough mountains
to climb with my eyes in the August heat haze.

FOUR RIVER SONGS

Stagalee

The only mountains near are tips that spill
black resin when it rains. Most of the trash
we make we live with. Fingers picking at limp
strings. The girls mostly go bad, then some
come good again. Nothing too new: Midnight Suzie,
Sarah Sleep Sundays. No point in going home

over the river, if a man could swim and not get
fish bit. Different's the way the fixings die here
on the tongue. Only the bottle burns just right.
Night in the steeltowns dirty as a mine. I'd walk
on water just to dance and hunt. Mostly I slide
and hope the weeds will someday take the streets.

No way I'd own what's tracking me. I'd work if I
could see the sense of shifting the stripped gears
of some old crone, or wearing dollars in a five cent
hatband, play Stagalee, the Bully of the Town, in
Cincinnati. Only the tunes run down abandoned lines
to the Ohio. What's Covington? What's lucky in Kentucky?

Sarah Sleep Sundays

End of the work week for us all. Whatever
men see in me they're always looking
backward. If I stand in your way, I say,
find a new track. I'm tired of doing time
for divers, miners, dreamers. One by one
turn up with blubber lips and loco eyes

out of the pitch black waters ... Haunts
sleepwalkers. I've got my own head now
furnished and paid for—maybe. Shawls won't
make me Queen of Sheba, nor a straw bonnet
any mountain schoolgirl. Honey, I've honey

of my own. Look for a bee tree but don't
shake my swarm. I'm what I want and where.
Whatever dirty sun comes sliding through

gray drapes finds me pure gold, winks
in a mirror, only haunts what's here.
You're doing fine, he says, believe me.

Rev. Philip Sax Annoyed By Angels

Amazing Grace—mighty unfitting in Gehenna.
Hell both sides of the river. Damned if you work
and twice damned if you don't. You grasp at drugs
and drink, beat children, walk into a knife, shoot
out the streetlights, anything that asks more of you

than you'd give. Once off your guard, I've had you
weeping that you're saved. Next day you hate me
way past the wives who knew you only halfway gone.
It's not the evil chokes you, but the good—"Good"'s
not the word, something like grit, glass splinters

in the foot; more of an irritant than inclination.
I've seen few of you die, yet buried scores. You
crawl into yourself, in beds, cells, corners—
keeping self-hate *that* pure. What I say Sundays
could have me wrestling angels if I let it get me.

Marty

Maybe it's being part Cherokee gives me the sense
of what I'm going to lose before they sneak land
off of me, or put my babies in the earth, pack off
half of my family one way, half the other. It helps
too, being fat. You can lie any way and where you light

looks permanent. You hold what's left, you make up
mountains; quilt, patchwork brighter colors to take
the dirt; scare out the scare with something scarier—
it works for men and children. You make a bear out
of the air, haunts, bugaboo—then sew on roses.

They fall asleep. You keep up half the night, your
lies your company, your tricks, the sense of being
fat Marty who makes them nettle coats. Blind
fiddler in the dark—whichever dark you choose.
It's fair, I guess, where pink hearts show the arrow.

OHIO, WINTER EDGE OF MORNING

Trees are strongly inked cracks despite
mists. Nothing is softened. Fog patches
stand still as cattle between bonewhite
barns and sunlight is washed-out crimson.

Back to Nature—but not this northern
border!—a hammer pounding your own nails,
crow echo exaggerating penultimate vowels,
sharp consonants of your own name across

an immense ploughland, crow-black. Here
straws stick out of earthclods, a khaki
army's advance, as if whole coalfields
were charging toward you demanding fire.

GEESE ON THE GENESEE

Two hundred rise from the glowing cornstalks
in black fields either side of the frozen Genesee
this red and white dawn. Their forming lines
open out, taking up the opal stare of the sky, each
wavering point in the chainlengths of geese drawn
North, clanking or honking to the far horizons, walls
of brass, distant Erie and Seneca. They go slowly,
adjusting their pace to a winter delayed past March,
crying out as if in protest against each individual,
unwavering fate that sets them flying always with
the pain of the wind, pinions plucked out, goose
skin shrill, heartbeat strained, one part of a hunger
more urgent than mating, skypull taut between Poles.

LAMENT FOR MARY MACLEOD

for Pipe Major Albert McMullin

It is the heavy rain again, playing
in the light shells of fallen leaves
these papery melodies, such distant
echoes of great northern seas

brown, clinkered cockleboats that ride
a gray and scarlet mosstide of these woods
you never knew, nor walked in, far from Skye

Good night, a brave *Goodnight*
Daughter of Scotland, so remote in time
the mists have finally claimed
all but your maiden name

you and your silvery shawl
held by a badger's claw
where random raindrops
gleam like garnets

gracenotes, dark burden of the pibroch's long
and alien strain, wailing to falling rain
in Appalachia now, unending late lament

OUR THIRD PRESIDENT

In the gardens of Monticello
                    little mountain?
                    sweet little mountain?
there is a sign
                    EXIT AND TOMB
and in Charlottesville
on the campus of the University of Virginia
a serpentine wall one brick thick
invention of Thomas Jefferson
third president and Cincinnatus
of the young republic
who under giant trees
and in an impressively ugly stone monument
sleeps
where brown tree frogs and green garden snakes
jump or skitter among the
large leaves
turned dark side up
and black bog earth
full of white threads

In all his inventions
a man must be faithful
to himself

"There is genius
even in his failures"
says one character of
another in
Thomas Love Peacock's novel *Gryll Grange*

There is a style in bringing forth a desk
or a clock or an unconventional house

also in writing a declaration or
designing a serpentine wall
that thinly meanders
only as intended

or in building a monument
which was not his invention

or in ordering a sign
which he did not intend
to be part of his garden

COURBET IN GEORGIA

Old Populist in a blue blouse
at times I took your canvas for the earth—
raw orange clay in the ravines, shrill green
of the new grapevine, deer red as rust
the kudzu almost blue

Any hour now they may expose you
for pocketing pink marble blocks
saved for the neoclassic tombs
of shyster smalltown tyrants

or claim the county's water rates and taxes
rise to the skies, the cardinals are rezoned
each time you're let out from museums
indigo buntings multiply in figtrees

What popularity you lack
your leaking, smelly pipe, your painters'-peasants' hands
your endless talk of good meat and potatoes
in everybody's pot, in every landscape
your kid's delight in bright bulldozers

LABOR DAY WEEKEND, NORTH GEORGIA

Thunder, the cardinal flower out by the creek
so rich a red in the cricket loud
cricket green weeds under a pewter sky.

Ticking from slashed mattresses and fawn
chicken feathers wander the yard
where roots wear through the stamped clay.

All the resources of emptiness are reached
in the corners of outbuildings. A calendar
from a funeral home is eight years out-of-date.

The nail it hangs by bleeds a long russet line
dividing Christ from the door he knocks on
in Jerusalem. Everything draws in

a perceptible second. Violence of rain.

BATHSHEBA COME MORNING:
A SHORT STORY IN FOUR VERSES

Characters: *John Mackay*
Toby, a dog
a moon bobbin

Carrion Crow Carrion

He wears beggar's ticks like broken arrows to the knees
of pale coffee corduroys, shooting the black
patches out of the sky—a terrible protest among
clouds. *Jeremiah.* Ostriches in the desert. It SHALL BE
a day of reckoning. And the dog slavers onto dry
kexies, anatomies, new sap for old, wound salve. A
crow comes down, breaking twigs—*Dies Irae.* Wind rising.

It is the bonnet of an old lunatic widowlady lost of
exposure ten years walking backwards in these trees—torn
mattress showing the springs of her ribs in hoarfrost.

Ah, God's cautious hand nests a sparrow. Counting, "One, two ..."
Also the hairs of John Mackay's head. Adulteries of love,
lower, under a brown pate, lie graying. How many fester
there like warwounds no dogslaver can salt or stay?—
The more pleasant the pain of old partings. And yet
a beautiful blue-black agate is a crow's eye fixing Mackay
that moment, grape dusty with darkness, dark bits of sky
overcoming all the queens in his head, he leaning over
counting already the white maggots quick in the crow.
        AMEN.

And Amen Also

Toby, the dog, worries his way into an underlife
of roots and rank earth sour with aftermath of
lynx piss, Styx water, the mummy wafts of old
leaves. Who has Egypt for a history? And a present
played out between white piles of hyena turds?—
Dark, territorial, claims. He relieves an itch,
old dogsbody, canine Cain, the root rakes him, excites
seven layers deep the sleepers. Throth rubs a peppery
oil on his lagging tongue. His eyes rheum over with
pleasure. Bitches drip gold. His master whistles.

His Master Whistles

Mackay hunts lights now in the thistle colored dusk
snapping the dog back with a shrill leash from holes
and the crows long gone in the gloom, or part of it.

Trucks bringing bootleg whiskey, white lightning, cold
taste of a mountain steam behind all that corn with
the sugar burnt into/out of it. Moonshiner Wade Erskin's

daughter, twenty years less Mackay's age, sweating the
quilt so it takes chill before dawn, the bed smelling
of bread. He rises and stretches. Wet air, sweet whiskey,

sour gutback recoil of guilt. His boots where he threw
them, an earlier Toby whimpering in a dream. And the girl
asleep in the dark, and no longer worth all the worrying—

once. Now, nine years aged in the wood, in the long memory
Wade Erskin's cow-eyed daughter, comes back a moon bobbin,
over the white pools of yarrow heads in the meadow—passes him.

Passes Him, Bathsheba Come Morning

Not for real, he tells himself, the bobbin gone down
to the smoking creek between cedars. And only a haunt
broke asylum like the widowlady that died of exposure
alone among litter of leaves and dead crows in the wood.

Bathsheba, filled with dead baby and shot, buried bearing
his child, died without speaking his name, and Erskin
crying like a dog when the men held him, lowering the gun

from her knees. What ghost out of Orcas, but *that* one
the sight of whose bare back and shoulders once broke him
fever and chills, times he'd walked into cobwebs in winter?

Now the rain rings the moon, and Bathsheba come morning,
Crows grown quiet in his head. Toby taking a dewbath.
Truck lights on the night run. "Can't you love me till morning?"
"Owl eye, crow eye. Can't you love me till morning … ?"

PART THREE

CABIN BETWEEN CREEKS

I   Lammas

Hum of summer and the blue fret of insects
over the goldenrod. She goes like a goosegirl
surrounded by white to hang sheets on a line
strung between gooseplums, blond pigtails arguing
over the blue checks of her shirt.

Whatever she's singing plays games in the head
where "Shady Grove" and a new ballad heard
on the car radio leapfrog. The singer and never
the song, pick-up tunes to an August monotony
cello bowing of grasshoppers, timpani

of the creek, where fat water idles, a Milky Way
of glitters, behind unmoving willows. No
way like noon while she stands there singing, pegs
a white square out in blue shadows of gooseplums—
fol-de-rol dawns and naked awakenings.

II   Samain

Old apple logs burn in the grate. At her mending
she curses the snapped thread, the poor light.
First snow falls on the meadow, white to white
on the yarrow heads, where a doe stands
quivering, not from cold, from the openness.

Nothing comes by the road from the gate, not
this evening. Against firelight her hair forms
a cave for her face, for her small breasts.
Concentration of everything on the thread.
Closed on herself she does not see the deer

know of the snow, or the meadow, or anything
outside the mending. Keeping the pageturn
quiet, the chairlegs, even breathing, quiet—
not to intrude on her curses all to herself
the ghosts, or the first snow, or the otherness.

III Beltaine

Green over gray. The creeks jingling as though
ice never slowed them. Mountains gather round
no longer dull rocks under sky. At mistlift
she climbs a logging scar by dogwood stars, finds
pink lady's-slippers among everyday wood sorrel.

She kneels, with long strokes brushes her hair
then lights a last fire in sunlight buttery
as log chinks. Day to set out the rockers, burn
dustdevils, shake blankets. Lost to all
counting time when the weather suspended it

brought back to tenantry, dates, decisions.
The cabin cleared, the car washed, the gas tank
filled. Nothing so catching as shrugs. She
unmakes the bed. She walks with an armload
of nights over warning floorboards.

DEER MOUSE

Small footfalls woke him to the trees
heavy with candles burning, runes
on the panes. He rose and dressed
quietly, closed the cabin door
quietly—corn husks on the plank steps.

Grass made tents in the meadow.
The isolate oak housed a shape
that might have been carved from basalt
except for the crescents, wound raw
on each wing. Mists banded the hills.

Fawn bullrushes, milkweed canes
creaked by the pond. Veins under ice
were blue lines in a woman's breast.
He stood in the unwarming sun. Wind
worried the power line. Nothing sang.

Locked out, locked in, too early
or maybe too late. Any day other
than this, he'd wake, lie an hour
in her breath, light a fire, read.
Leaves of the pond set in layers,

he stared into other woods. In a
bootprint, its white belly pressing
the paws of the deer mouse pushed
upwards. The eyes that he saw were
unscareable, loving as hers through ice.

THE PIERCE POEMS

Place:	*A farm in North Georgia*
Characters:	*Pierce*
	Ms. Marbillon, the visitor
	Pierce's Mother
	Pierce's Father
	A Raccoon
	Rhode Island hens

Visits

Their California guest rocks and says:
"I grew up in the desert. I was a hawk watcher.
Sometimes I see the sky as a set of wings.
One thing you can bet on. God's not pleased
with what's going on in Washington." And Pierce
watches the rainstones ricochet on cans,
Rhode Island hens peeking out through spokes
of the wheels, wonders to himself how long
she's come here to roost, bringing wet weather,
keys out of *Daniel*, who can spy Anti-Christ
in your eyes, hold a courthouse on the porch
for politicians, Blacks, Jews—all the bad news

out of the Bible and newspapers. A half-dollar
won't buy nothing in the store. His dumb parents
put up with too much for the sake of some cousin's
ex-wife out of nowhere. And only last night
in the light from windows, it went through their
trash again. Maybe God's a raccoon, Pierce thinks
an old-fashioned bandit with manners, picking the good
from the bad with fine, ladylike gestures, laughing,
to itself, all nerves; a bit high on luck.

Pierce's Hat

Pierce watches his father flay
the pelt from the unbelievable
pink underside of skunk, a hat
for him. He'll look like a girl.
He's already worried about his smell.

He knows what Ms. Marbillon—taking
her maiden name—thinks of them
all—she from the civilized West—
dumb mountaineers, only she says
"cretin," French, for some way

of looking at things too high, Moon
mania, loco, left standing behind
the door when the brains were
give out. It don't figure if you
can multiply or divide, you're done

by what hick bit of God's earth you
come from. Only, he'll wear that hat
to please Pa, who thinks he's pleased
to be Daniel Boone, buy the whole sky-
line of Eden from some dumb Indian.

Pierce Gives Ms. Marbillon An Arrowhead

A present—of sorts—from the savages
to rest among bright pins on the frayed
cushion, heart shaped, in the dark.
Give us, God, nothing we can't use,
an embarrassment from the enemy.

The excuse of the Good Pagan has worn thin.
This is an idol of one kind or another,
a war god, a sliver of hand-worked stone.
Earth has redeemed the blood. Beware
of gifts that cost the giver nothing.

The Ark of History is overcrowded.
It's high time for a new Flood. "Per-
adventure there be one … " Rocking, rocking,
crooning Deborah's hymn to the hens.
There are no rafts on that water.

Pierce Upset

When they say "upset", he thinks of himself
as tipped out of a baby carriage, a tantrum
only his father's belt can put right. He looks
at his father and thinks of Isaac. No ram
appears for him under the rafters of the barn.

"I'll teach you manners—you 'Ma'am' a lady … !"
She lays stripes on him. *She* is at the heart
of his pain. Pa is only the handyman. He weeps
for them both, howls more than he need do.
It is Pa who stands upsidedown in the doorway.

Ms. Marbillon Leaves

Whoever hears has heard—prayers, curses,
putting a chicken hand in the earth by the door,
the fingers cut off, only one left, pointing. Ms.
Marbillon is going. Plainly the gains from the
Godless are like cornbread caught in the throat.
She damns them with terrible smiles. They are sure
to be hearing from her from one marriage cousin's
house or another. She loves them all equally.

To Ma, "she's lonely, poor thing" in a freed kitchen.
Pa tramps the house like the yard. Pierce is lost
in a frogpond stupor—everything ugly, ug-ly!
The dumb hens haven't missed their dead. The rain
raises rivers each hour, but the mountains are higher.

VI
Counting the Grasses

THE WELL

Watching you run
under the sprinkler
I know how good it is
to have an aging body

yours
tightening to points or
over graded planes, mine
showing off
the weathers and
well-being of years

scars, slacks, but
in no way divided
from my eyes
I would not deny
its history

going down a little
in its own good time
as yours
ripening
springs up

Look
we meet at the well
my daughter
in the sunlight
of spread water
on wet grass

we dance the double dance
of the lucky seeds

either the coming together
of a moment
of some unstressed
movement
of the years

MAGNOLIA

Look at the bees in the magnolia
they pick it to pieces
They satisfy

The polished cup of a leaf
keeps all the falling pieces
at each bit it dips
like a bird's beak
tapping time

The magnolia blossom
was white this morning

When we got up
it was white

It hurt our eyes
it was so white

It was as white
as our new kitchen

Now it is nine o'clock
All the bits in the cup are brown
There is a black stump
on the bough above
The bees
are not interested

Hurry, hurry to have breakfast!

Then what shall we do?
Yes, what shall we do?

Run about kissing each other—
And laughing
Yes, laughing

Laughing and kissing
each other

Kissing each other
and laughing

Yes, kissing and laughing
in the sunlight
now

OSPREY

A bird calls "Jay-Jay-Jay-Jay" over and over from the far gate.
In the meadow, a thousand pale flecks take the glare
without the movement of water. Vines at the cabin door
complicate inane shadows.

All this the osprey skims, appearing out
of nowhere, without announcement.

Effortlessly—his great notched wings
lazy, completing each beat a little late—
he opens something like windows
between the noon blue mountains
and the closest trees.

CEDAR WAXWINGS DRUNK ON BERRIES

Photographed in a white sweater
against March light, against a wall of maps
I give my image, my terra incognita
of forty-seven years, unsmiling
to the photographer

Perhaps, as the primitive think
this is altogether too much giving away
a playing with souls. It is not Samoa
or New York State that is diminished
in the camera

And all over the garden
the cedar waxwings
are drunk on holly berries
They chatter in dogwood boughs
clowning for one another
or dunk yellow and gray tails
in the birdbath
and may not make it North

CATSPAW

All morning two mockingbirds
have been trying to divebomb the cat,
but the cat has the barberry shrub
between it and the murderous beaks.

Noon, the cat is warily half asleep
in the cool shadow of the bush,
one bird continues with a shrill scream
attacking ineffectually out of the sun.

"Kamikaze", the cat says with a drowsy purr,
"little gray and white kamikaze.
I am the carrier you never sank
between Guam and the Coral Sea.

"When I am ready to do so,
out of a catspaw of cloud
I will bring down another sun
to darken your bright and inscrutable eye."

GOOD FRIDAY, 1978

Along the line of least resistance
I sit in a book-filled room and read nothing
watching through windows the sticks of the fig tree
awaiting the first birdsfoot of light green

I wonder at the many ways the Chinese had
for expressing distance and intimacy
the abstract mountains, a foreground of fruit trees

Here the quince is in bloom, and so many years of marriage
have brought us what we least expected
intimacy and distance

Tired of the furor of writing, I accept distances
Next week our dogwood will flower
Today, the buds are hard pellets of beaten tin

Along the line of least resistance
I think of some minor Great Man of the East
an exile from courts, a retired poet
or an exiled poet and retired courtier

He journeyed many months to the place of his birth
married the least likely girl in the village
a deaf mute, a child, a peasant, and lovely

So he settles down to make more children in silence
At night, now, he swims with a tiny wife who only sighs
By day, he feeds chickens in an old shed—
the ways of chickens are brutal, ask any smallholder

How many hours are filled with gazing into mist
listening to beaks chipping on stones, bird bickering?
How many days for the smell of rain falling on dust
chicken dung, cinders, tall nettles by a stone tub?

The chatter and manners of the courts are not forgotten
How can he smother forever the insistent words of his poems?
It is harder, he thinks, to fill the quiet hours with quiet ...

Then breaks off, with no need now for comparisons

SUNDAY MORNING

Trying to kill a quail
the cat had savaged
on Sunday morning

Becoming at once
the cat's accomplice
only the cat was by a small margin
the more efficient
though he had meant
to have a whole morning's murder
out of it

It was like the Duke of Monmouth's
execution
fifteen chops
with an apology
between each chop
"My Lord, forgive me …"

and the quail writhing alive
stretching out long, long, scaled legs
to each blundering blow

It was no fit business
or prayer

and the orange clay off the spade
making only a mess
of curled feathers
like small shavings
from a dozen different colored woods

all that neatness, that careful distinction
mauled in the one ball

the defiant and agonized eye
muddied over and out

"my Lord—or Lady—forgive me."

TREE STRUCK BY LIGHTNING

The tiny starburst
lit fusewire
touches the trunk
and the tree turns over
dies to the last twig.

This is not a sequoia
with defense systems
for everything except
axe and saw
but a hundred-foot oak.

In mid summer
every leaf browns in weeks
against white lake water
and the green green of cypress.

The tree is unstable
at once becomes danger
to a vast circumference

and the boring begins,
silent insects, the rap-tap
of woodpeckers, backward
carpenters on a listing scaffold.
And the rain revives nothing.

In the sodden wood
of lichen and Death Caps
some weak aftermath endures
tweaks the nose like candles snuffed.

IN PRAISE OF OUR DAYS

His poetry would be called epic
only by fellow Boeotians
This is the stuff sparrows pick up
building a nest, the excitement
of breaking the seals
of newly-baked bread

And truly the earth bestows its own kind
of good luck to those
who mention bathers in dust baths
and mud baths
the frozen organpipes of ice
under the banks of ditches in winter

and never a word of Antaeus, Earth's son
Boreas blowing, or anything of the sort
Yet a kind of epicure
after all of precise effects
is required to record
in chaste dactyls
beaks picking up polished grain
from a tin tray

or to leave ever after
an unstressed image
plain glamor of words
four jackdaws shivering
in the spring rain

MEADOW GRASS

for Marie Mellinger

There is more to this meadow under the mountains than mere names
of fescue, blue Timothy, panic grass, foxsedge, hopsedge—but my eyes
keep coming back to the dark strokes of plantain, each head as if surrounded
by a ring of pale insects, a curious, almost ugly crown

The Cherokee called these weeds "Footprints of Englishmen"—
wherever the settlers went the plantain grew, broad leaves
escaping under their heels, the wayward wagon tracks
grew like dark stars on the banks of a Devon lane
seen here against clay of the same colors: oxblood to orange
foxbrush, fernseed, the outrageous rust of men
washed into creeks in the runoff of heavy rains
mingling Greek blood and Trojan
like Scamander in the old tale
some settlers had by heart, and more never heard of

The roots of red flowers went to the chiefs and warriors
Yellow and white were squaw flowers, went to the mending of women
Children sucked on the creeping stems of the pea plant and grew eloquent
in a language that no longer mattered. It was the settlers' names
that caught up with the changing meadows—wort, balm, and bane
Gerard and Culpeper claimed them

Not the Seven Bark, nor the lovecharm Pipsissewa profitted
in the eclipse of the Sun Spirit and the Star Maiden
only the transplanted plantain—spear, vinegar sponge, corona of insects—
only the Deptford Pink, Venus's Looking Glass, Mouse Ear ...
The weed-strong invaders clung like pea plant to the alien clay

I would escape a moral if I knew how
or remake one if I could stop my wandering
The grass changes under my feet. Words, names, change in my mouth
under a shifting, mostly indifferent sky

HOMESTEAD

I

I woke to the strong smell of skunk, something under the floorboards
and took up my troubled thoughts where I'd left them, the feeling
these fields wouldn't pay back taxes, the too few students, those
who cancelled at the last minute, those who never wrote or came
Something was slipping away from us, little by little, with no one
to stop it, no single idea to hold back the developers who had ideas
of their own. It looked like the last chance on the clock face

Mice skirmishing the trash in the kitchen, two screech owls far off
in the woods. I opened a window not knowing whether the skunksmell
would rush in after me or be diminished by that. It seemed better

The house was full of presences, mostly good ones, so much living
had gone into the wood, so many worriers there before me, less those
workers who hadn't anything left at the day's end to fret with. The wind
came up the meadow. Something distanced the creeks. One lightning bug
looped the loop past the windowpanes. Whatever was doomed didn't know it

It's an old story, maybe. And who'd sat up all night with bug lamps
putting poultices on the throat of a burning child? Who'd added up the
price of seed corn on the back of an envelope? Who'd wanted things with
an ache? I wasn't counting my company. What comforts the teething or
the dying out of an old house creaking, easing itself in the wind? Prayers

promises, voices, I.O.U.s—an old story, dispelled, somewhat, by the breeze
in any crib made by hands that can't hold forever. No, we never said we
could either, only thought it, a bit of faith—a lot more pig-headedness
Run for the Granny woman, tell Preacher we've got something we held back
to tell him. What's left us but a mess of weeds and the same words? Nobody
liked the moral much either, so much sorrow and joy going
                                                into the good wood going

II

No, that isn't it either, or it's only part of it. Tonight
reading Pliny in the old house—so many wonders, so many
marvels! The white nights of moths, punctuation of wings

So many smells, ploughland, the perfumed earth; setting each
flower apart, or counting the grasses; aftertaste and deep
strangeness of wine, old Falernian, scuppernong, muscadine

all the earthworm turns over, a powder of wood along sills
under the holes of post beetles, the scraping of paper-wasps
doorhandles, the back of a chair, so many wonders—

what I leave of me holding the book too hard, my heels
lightly drumming the floorboards, beat of those wings
all the burning going into the eyes, a bruising of surfaces

I sink deeper into dark waters by night than those waterlillies
Pliny talks of on the Euphrates, to float up by day out of
nowhere, a face from the floor of dreams, the sunboat of Ra

III

Maps, tracks across oilcloth; hours pass, the wind
turns pages, the book forgotten; what I read there
nothing, except where it recalls certain moments, or
certain sensations—dormant seed in the forest floor

Thomas Browne, Pliny, Virgil, poet of exiles, all
the things men hold to in those dark hours before
dawn, the necessary dark, the quiet of the Moon
Silente luna, old Roman in the mountains of Rabun
a ritual of taxes, tithes, troubles, the tick tack of an insect

IV

But we were the uprooted anyway. Weren't we always in exile
with England in the map of the mind growing smaller and smaller
or Scotland, or Ireland—Wales, Denmark, Germany … wherever
there were hearths, fields to be deserted, gray cities by estuaries?

It wasn't the Mothers of North Europe, was it, who wanted
their children, those restless sons, always about them?

Wild geese, wanderers, with irreconcilable ideas, religions
we came, we saw, we were conquered, an old tale, and the
land lust led us astray, our possessions possessed us
We carried the lumber of Europe to one breakdown place after
another, one hollow, one dry creekbed, one dusty arroyo

When the books spilled down the hill a small bird watched us
When the mice got the sheet music we were fast asleep
When a dog bark parted the night I considered my hands

V

I have made a start after all. I have accepted the tilt of this table
having moved it from floorboard to floorboard. I have mended my writing
as a plough follows the contours of a hill. "Geography dictates" even
in small things. That's it, of course, a lesson that seemed worth learning—
where the grain goes. There appeared little point in deciding whether water
shaped the rock, or the rock sculptured the water. It was all one, a flowing—
in certain rockpools, a marriage. It is not a matter of compromise either
Earth doesn't bother with terms like Who-were-they?—Indians? Only a slim line
I hold onto and dare not drop: furrow, grain, contour, thread, cardinal line
Or say rather I have given myself over at last to the wood,
                                                a simple ceremony

VI

Invaders, intruders resentful of later invaders. And what
after all, is a "homestead"? Something in place of a home?
Maybe. Some Government grant to the homeless and landless
out of the lands of others, some yellowing title deed, to be seen
ironically enough, under glass in the Cherokee Museum, giving
this horizontal and that, looking neat as a piece of a quilt, to the
tune of so many acres, and earned over so many years of labor by
God fearing, after a fashion, and, certainly, white, people, having
a say and a vote, and then, feudal after the fact, having the right
and the duty to bear arms in battle, in defense of the homestead

Thomas Hopper, you who got lost somewhere in the War, the only
war that matters, the one that divides the heart and the heartland
Sam Hopper, you who shaped the poplar beams of this ark riding
the night, what you left keeps the same distance between creeks
is weathertight still and upright. Thomas Hopper, still lost

And you who planted the gooseplum should know it bears fruit
in odd years, only leaves in even. Likewise, the garden walled
with stones like a stockade gives us wild garlic and fleabane
The creek nearest the cabin is full of watercress, all stalks

Left to himself in winter, the ratsnake under the floorboards
feeds off the last ears of Indian corn and keeps down mice
that revive miraculously, perhaps by spontaneous generation
out of dustdevils, lint, hairpins, that fall through the cracks
to multiply each summer the snake is scared off, intruded on

VII

God of Thunder, rumble of storms, rumble of rockers, stray rifle shots
Joe Pie Weed, or Queen of the Meadow, lashes the windowpanes
with the rain. I sit long awake smoking, listening for messages
not meant for me, returned "Addressee Unknown", "Try a different
mountain." Before the storm, dust made a moonscape of the laurel
you called "ivy" along roads. When I close my eyes I am walking
the creekbed colored with yellow butterflies. The long war goes on
Strangers to ourselves, we turn upon strangers. The weeds ride again
to the windows, livid horsemen of lightning with a smear of purple

Only the company of the dead is tamed of all violence. We can still
wrap you up like old letters, send you back in the wood, or we think
we can. So we're doing fine, just fine, only help us to hold on
hold on to these fields, these weathered boards, these man marks
you made for yourselves, or unknowingly. Keep faith with the floundering
Walk back through the wet, tall weeds in the mists of the morning
From your wars, or whatever, return.
                    Give us the title cleared, the deed intact

HALF LIGHT

I mistook a dead pine down
at the edge of the meadow
for smoke, thought of the forest
burning. There were white daisies
trapped in the gray haze

Often Sam Hopper walks this road
his big stick scattering the stones
"Go in," I thought, but waited
He has pulled down too many horizons
under the brim of his hat

OBJECT

Long yellow legs like those of a chicken
are working up-creek against the current
close to the bridge. Those loose joints
jerk and reset. The limbs are raw meat.

Chimera that shows no head. The body
bumps against roots, rolls widdershins, spins—
gray and black mat of what looks like weeds,
inert, already dead, where the legs are urgent, alive.

My daughter and I, elbows on the railing
gaze down into water and shadow, our different
nightmares each in some close way confirmed
this Midsummer's Evening, and do not speak.

HAWKS

Hawks are the cats of the air, their
squalling and mewing, their
slow stalk, a shadow sliding
over the shorn field, their
pounce, the talons
locked into something alive
the deathgames
hardly begun

SCYTHIA

"Rumors Grow Easy in Clayton"
— sign on the K-way wall in Clayton, Ga.

"Of course most people read Latin in those days"
— Mary Russell

No workman who knows wood, the mysteries of grain,
would shingle with cedar under an August moon, however
behind-hand the work. This is the growing time
of gourds, the vegetable garden overrun with snakes
hissing for water, the green tendrils drawing up
hidden streams from the rock. Even the fishermen,
two figures who stand like figures of lava in the
mid-flow of a low creek, are watching their wrists,
divining in time of drought. A rumor too strong to suppress,
the urgency of insatiable bodies, releases the yeast of
fields, shakes down the dust from the beebalm.

Catullus, Propertius rant of the raw power that held them
slaves, unlike the slick Ovid, who had remedies for everything
except the bitterness of exile. Their beds are cold. Only
the odors of love are immune to the moonlight, the supposed
amnesia of death. No gossip reaches us from Rome. But what
Scythian, what spindle-shanked hoyden of the mountains
turns over coins or tea leaves, then rubs her small breasts
with unguent, prepares anew the old spell under an August moon?

FENCE SHADOWS

Nothing much is going to change
the clumps of yarrow, but in five minutes
the fence shadows will reach them
I can't judge the difference until it happens
and staring will only put me to sleep

Two girls are coming up Betty's Creek
trying to catch butterflies
but not trying hard enough, laughing
Someone in cities is wishing he were here
And I'm wishing ... Oh, well, nothing much

GRIST MILL

I was thinking today of the Bible, of the
"pearl of great price", and I wondered
who threw it away and where—the pearl
I mean, not the good woman, wife, the
other side of the metaphor—

perhaps into a millpond. The sky here
was the color of old oyster shells. In July
it was like a warm spell in winter, the same
lighting, the rust on gray wood, the pale
yellow of mash, of sand on the creek bottom

Even the trees seemed to have shed their leaves
for a moment only, just till some bird I
didn't know the name of came flitting
from bank to bank, as if he'd caught up
the wind clamped in his beak to start
the day stirring again. I thought

of the woman now, of a woman no less
lovely than the earth in this hour, pearl
purl, or the other, Latin, name for a
sea jewel. All the time that the water
and stone ground up white pearls of corn
I was turning names over, wondering

how any man could be that much of a fool, or even
that if a man grew that perverse he'd do better to
tie a millstone round his own neck and throw
himself in, not the pearl. I thought of
those quiet, dark waters of the millpond
imagining cloud where no cloud passed in the sky

CLOUD CLIMBER

"The Cherokee lived in the rich, fertile valleys, but gathered their medicine plants from the mountains. Certain sacred plants, such as the red spruce and fraser fir of the higher elevations, could be gathered only by a certain Adowahi, known as the Cloud Climber."
— Marie Mellinger

When I came down from the ridgetop
a stray dog was watching itself in the creek
a blacksnake came out of the orange swamp

I was not altogether ready for the sunlight
a bough of dewberries, the glistening horseflies
or the bright nailheads in the fallen schoolhouse

Last Chance, the school was called. I took a chair
out of the fetid room with half a floor, and sat there
peeling the stick that took me up and down the mountain

I'd walk away from words and walked all morning
and half the afternoon. Without intention
I'd crossed the State line into Carolina

Cow bells were jangling somewhere and I wondered
how it would be to have a bell always about you
and thought of thoughts, that lifelong irritation

Somewhere up on the ridge the spell was broken
I'd brushed against a herb, or picked a leaf
and gone on walking, never knowing the difference

but sensing that the day had changed. The grass
the trees, were just the same in Georgia and in Carolina
and on the gray boards of the school some boy had knifed in "Hello Florence"

NOTES FOR A JOURNEY

Lake Russell, Georgia

I

The larches flicker cut off the waterlights in a lower key of the
eyes as between branches a white-tailed deer turns heavily and is
off heavily with more noise than expected opening the wood before
her a gully halfway up which the brown of fallen leaves turns to
astonishing lush green of moss and blue strokes of a herb I do not
know a catch in the wind it is the weather it is a breath also
of something sharp sweet indrawn and released as though through an
open mouth this is part of a landscape I also inhabit it with more
than the deer going ahead opening the wood before us there are
more tracks here than deer cutting a leaf with a hoof sending some
fragrance into the air upsetting the patterns of the almost still
day I go on and my feet make a noise on the white crust of lichen
decay on small fallen twigs but also I grope back as sound travels
all ways at once the smell is no more to be found except as I remember
it but my nostrils are expectant sensing it must come again as if
too I was walking many woods at once for the sharp scent of seconds
opened up further or back where the deer lost sight of before me leads

II

Reading Yeats out loud by the fireside the hearers add one stick after
another the fire licks out to meet the sticks there is almost a
meter in the sound of the sap exploding any way I walk from here
I will entangle my head in the webs strung from the tall trunks of
pine the moon unable to get into this clearing that is a clearing
only because the pines are so tall and have no branches for twenty
or thirty feet from the ground is on the lake beyond the bushes
as white as it might be on a road or a roof flat mat surface it does
not glitter it is water only because I know it is water because the
lake is there and the moon finds it to coat it is almost the same
set pattern as the snake one of us killed and hung belly upwards
in the poison ivy and hazel bushes beside the trail but away from
the children it will change as slowly all night as the snake changes
a frog croaks and a car comes over loose gravel under the burden of
the poem the ranger walks down to talk lights his pipe a pause is
made in the reading a cone of ashes falls off the log end into the fire

III

Someone is going unseen with a lantern seen through the trees breaking
the webs rocking the patterns of the trunks as if this were all
water we were under the children yawn watching the lantern go up
path away the ranger shakes hands twice in the time he talks with
us goes off after awhile to the parked car where his wife has been
waiting the book is picked up I begin again as the lamp comes back
through the woods and the trees rock smoke from the fire moves curling
around the legs of the table our legs and in the poem too there is
talk of the play of shadows as a new smell comes with the firesmoke

IV

Most are asleep under the picked up peaked covers of tents the axe
is chocked into the long log that still burns the moon is no further
on in the sky the fire occasionally tries bits of the poem or matter
less easily put into the words something is shaking itself quietly loose
in the woods as if the restraint of a vine were irksome the least
tether expendable whatever starts now has the hours until morning
to go as far off as it can all things opening before it gather behind

NASTURTIUMS

The plot of fat green leaves
the scarlet and orange flowers
must be lifted
from the blades of the mower

it is the smell
rank as origin
more pungent
than the bean flower
without eroticism
unadulterated
from the root

sunlight does nothing
but strengthen
the white alum

these flowers
are too open for trumpets
but beware, bees
something there is here
deceptively obvious

ambrosia of the immortals

and where are the old gods now?

ZINNIAS

Vision of Dante, Tintoretto, Titian
a corona of stars, Ariadne's ring
but not on blue, constellation, but
in the scarlet center of the zinnia
these bright yellow starflowers
the Sisters' unmazy dance, the complete
and completing: "Ashes, ashes; we all fall"
                                          up

SNAPDRAGON

A hidden bee
makes the snapdragon speak

its purple jowls
masticate sound
and also silence

in a tented bier
pompe funebre
of mulberry velvet
something murmurs awake

Merlin's prophecy perhaps

tremble, Wales

guard the Marches,
Albion!

SILENT TRADE

I envy the actor's voice
the dancer's gesture
Silence leaves all suspended
it is decent
not decay

ending a line with a period
or cutting in with a comma

nothing made to last
commands the luck of the living

you come in with your eyes
alter much
and the meaning is mended
extends in your life
as it ends
whatever was starting here

A child asked to define
"What's poetry?" wrote
"It's made of clay but holds water"

how shall we break that crock
and yet give form to the flow

all possible shapes in air
and no poem named between us

THREE WISHES

Even as I write
a hard white shell
is forming
round each black word

Even as you weave
the knots go out
from you
and are locked
in the pattern

How shall we defy
the undoing all of the done?

Is it by asking
three wishes
in the old way

hazard
unhappiness
fear?

To keep words
as themselves
wriggling in water
or burnt out
in the sun

To bring back
each knot you tie
to the living thing

COUNTING THE GRASSES

Something dies off in a poem the days after
as though these words weren't the painted wings
of butterflies, but those of dragonflies
that returned their light. Ephemeral—
what a beautiful word for what goes out of words!

I can't hold it. The mist rack spilling off mountains
the jerky strides of crows in the stubble
I shrug my shoulders. What's left but the morning?

On white sheets of paper I spread out the grass stems
blow off the loose pollen, affix the glue
touch the meadow with my hands, the accounted-for meadow
Only a fly is there to be interested
walking over the wet ink of my notes

SASSAFRAS

How they brought the bark of sassafras
to brew tea for the throats of chimney-sweeps
in eighteenth-century England—no, it's too
fanciful to see those soot-black boys in
Blake's poems released into an Eden
of American trees, who choked, trapped
in the brick stacks, saw a square of gray
sky only, above them, died among birdbones
dreaming of sunlight yellow as sassafras

THE FLY

Into a square of sunlight the transparent wings
green veined, the lacquered body blue bronze
shines like old ink

match of the moment
hesitation in midmorning

the drone life song
a cleaning of long legs

phosphorous flare and smoke
alights anywhere
old Lucifer
but one of Beelzebub's

eyes me as I it
yet from honeycombed bulges
am I gray or broken lights
of the Adam window?

so to it, so me
no moral but the mere presence

it is September when flies die
ornate period
on two blank pages

DRAGONFLY

Dragonflies have confused memories

What lights them, what colors them
went out eons ago

They only
are the half-brothers of stars

VII
"Having No True Grief, No History"
(The Mask Of History)

BEGGAR FROM THE NORTHERN SHIRES

I know no other land
Than these storm laden hills
Where sheep cower among granite folds,
But the rain finds them still;
Where the plover nests among stones
And the curlew cries peevishly,
Piping now and again and shrill,
Having no true grief, no history.

I stand by the Old House,
Dry, in a crook of the wall,
With the gate broken open and wait
For the Moss Trooper's call,
And hear hooves in the empty yard
And cries the winds blow
Over the stacks like smoke with a fall
Of soot like black snow.

Three windows open South
Without glass or wall between
But the mist curling over the slate
And a road as white as a stream ...
The lambs lie down in the hills
And I crouch by the ruined gate
While the rook packs scatter and cry
Spectres lost in the mists and late.

CONQUISTADORES

No more the white gods of the shore,
Their faces bear the scabrous rind
Of fruit long ruined in the sun,
Pecked at by all the birds of war.

Into the lush and yielding lands
They drive, these hundred men of steel;
Where feathered armies rise in flight,
Toy cities crumble in their hands.

Their foemen recognize and fly
These stalking horses of a plague,
The scourge of some insatiate god,
No gift of blood can pacify.

Not one of them now thinks of Spain,
Nor of the boats, burned long ago;
Cased in his armor and alone
Each serves one leader, greed, for gain ...

To span that continent with haste,
And wrest, before the fever wins,
The final burden in his grasp
Of all gold Mexico laid waste!

QUETZALCOATL

This bride of corn whose fragrant hair
The wind has mapped upon the air,
This bride of water whose cool hands
Are pressed by cloud upon the land
Call forth the fisherman whose net
Was cast across the Silver River,
In whose meridian shoulders met
The twin bolts of an Aztec quiver.

What is the sheen of horsemen's metal
In the dark passes of the night,
Or serpents' scales that in the deep
Turn of a sudden to the light
To that red gold beneath the earth
The Spaniard missed; that glows again
Under the heaving of the corn
And the wild weeping of the rain?

NEWS FROM SYRACUSE

Showing only their heads as yet above the swaddling,
Breathing the scented air, aware of pulling steel,
Their flesh confirmed as flesh and stroked by danger,
Five councillors through currents of sensation
Surface toward the waiting civic day—
Papers and sub-committees and the anxious clients—
Their formal mind reclaimed, their word becoming law ...

What interruption to expect—looked-for assassins
In such retreats? Guards at each barber's door,
Or parent gods prevent—*Now*, on this instant, such intrusion—
Covered with blood, looms up Medusa, rumor headed,
A hundred-fold in glass, this one surviving boy
Turning your world to stone with his 'Defeat!' 'Defeat!'

THE EARL OF ARUNDEL

"He was a man supercilious and proud, who lived always within himself, and to himself, conversing little with any who were in common conversation; so he seemed to live as it were in another nation . . ."
— Clarendon

Drawn to Greek stones, intaglios, busts, rings,
Pride, patronage, apprentice princes, kings;
My gallery's aswarm, none living, by;
Medicis let their banking slip, so I
Drop England's business and Vandyking still
Keep council in the Council, smile, and will
Plot paradise for one. Your words, your war,
Scarce trespass on me now; then, close the door.

QUAKER ELLWOOD

Ignore one head for hydras, like the Quaker Ellwood
who saw the drawn and quartered in a Newgate cupboard:
Tongue, Philips, Gibbs, all parboiled together
with cummin seed and bay salt to withstand the weather
and blackbirds' beaks while they were lecturing London

on treason—or the poor pretense of flesh
to keep its colors in a turncoat season.
First in a basket black with coaldust
then in a kettle streaked with orange rust ...

O, jostled in the Jordan of the waters
come forth as innocent as calves' heads from the cauldron.
Three bristly, blotched albinos rise where Ellwood beckons.
"Begot that moment an abhorrence in my nature ..."
of what must melt in time in Thames, in any river.

WOLSEY

These nights I sleep the deeper for the cold
and dream I go sleepwalking like a Jeremias
at Fountains, maybe, through an open quarry,
great purple drums and purple stands of loosestrife,
ragweed, where squirrels in their original vair
make up the choirsong's absence, Bedlam nuns
over a rosary of nuts chatter a Nunc Dimittis
to the blind, cobwebbed windows filled with hills,
ripe with a yellow mist, crushed apples, mold.

God, or some country boy, clacks the leper's rattle
down the long rides of stone for a Good Friday
that outlaws Easter. All England laid under a Bull
of Excommunication signed by no pope in Rome—
Where's Rome? But then again, where's England?
A wind from Thule, great lords of greed to pick
a shrinking carcass. Everything gone. These hundred
doomsday tombs like Fountains spread over acres.
Stones rolled away. No man-God risen.

I stir at cockcrow. On the counterpane are thirty
silver pieces stamped with familiar Caesar, Henry ...
Or do I sleep, shift from one stone vault to another?

ENGLISH HISTORY POEM

England's obsessed with brave defeats:
We've done Dunkirk to death,
Mons and Corunna
And all that fabled lot—
But what of victories?

All the while
Unnoticed rode our fleet
Off Africa—"God
Damn your freedom of the seas!"
Britannia's right of search.
Yankee and Portuguese,
All slavers turned about.

Pure altruism with hard heads;
They broke the bondage
That their fathers built
With sense, and precious little
Sense of guilt.

Ruined West Indian trade,
For which Lord Nelson shadowed Villeneuve
And left all England open to attack.

They, long ago, then Lincoln, freed the Blacks.
Mansfield's Decision, not Dred Scott,
Should set dates straight.

And all that effort was supplied from tills
Filled by the brutal labor of the poor
In Lancashire—that's irony!—
Young children chained to looms
Have set slaves free.

Our history's all confused:
Cold Pitt providing armies
To the Fiend
To fight against   *
Free Tyranny's excesses ...

Perfidious Albion—
Perfidious to herself.

The mean shopkeepers
So often closing shop
For sentimental good ...
Is that the point?
I wish I knew.
I wish I knew my country's nature
As you do.

PORTRAIT

How to disguise the body's history
She studies in a glass as green as Wales;
And with a skill older than alchemy
Freezes her seasons under falls of snow.

No accident could trespass in her hair,
Nor lift the mask with one malicious cry:
When she must turn to meet her lover's stare
Her eyes are freed like mirrors from their past.

REPORTED MISSING

I hit, lovingly, all the Homeric chords,
Hector's farewell to Andromache,
a backdrop of cut stone, an alley
by the Skaian Gate, so long ago,
and maybe all pure myth.

The Dean's note on the desk
says that you won't be there,
and yet you are,
a pale face in the furthest row
against the wall,
hair wrenched back in a knot,
severe, taut, seemingly attentive.

What am I telling you
this January morning
of unexpected sunlight
harder than armor?—

Astyanax in tears
of terror at his father's
coxcomb plumes, but black,
one all-engulfing wave
of war ... Astyanax, small bones
cracked on the walls ...

(What frightened you
last night?) ...

or Hector's laugh,
courage beyond the reach
of any god, or half-god
like Achilles;

or Andromache's eyes,
like yours perhaps,
slaves in men's senseless lives,
taught a heroic art?

TO MY NEIGHBOR AND ALMOST NAMESAKE
SHOT BY STRANGERS WHILE WALKING HIS DOG
AND AMONG HIS FLOWERS

The loss I admit is soon lost.
Each day a *Constitution* or a *Journal*
Lies on the lawns that grow for the mowing.
Now dogwood distracts from the burnt azaleas.

None of your money was taken with your life.
Bleeding away through twenty hours,
You were able to identify your assailants,
Though none was known to you before that morning.

Perhaps the color of their eyes was singular;
Triggered your mind the instant that they shot you,
As you reached back behind you for your wallet,
Knowing you had to pay for unexpected visits

But not how much. We had missed meeting
Exactly by a letter and one street.
Friends who mistook z for a t rang up,
Were reassured and left congratulations.

Grieved, I was not, nor much ashamed by luck;
Moved for a moment that moved on—new flowers,
My house in a dead-end street,
And no dog to walk in the early hours.

MARIANNE

Under the helicopter's belly lie
the fields of France
this August afternoon

The harvesters look up
for sound that bores
like other reapers
this time through the sky

For us a double stitching hems
the patchwork rust
ocher and cinnamon of crops

Two snakelike lines
meander into haze
dark green and only certain yards apart
their shrubs throw back a lesser show of light

Cast skins of Teutoburg and Troy
the hiding
forming place of men
divided into tribes

Godlike if we peruse
 fields also diced with stones
Half of a cross
moves darkly from our craft

Lone calvaries by roads
"La Chant de Craonne" and "Madelon"
echoes in the stirred air
our cutting blades cut through

Quickly to Paris
Four long years of war
now sixty more

The sky remade as sky
The scars
an elemental absence
holding on

VALTELLINA, 1945

In Milan
a man hangs upside down
from a meathook
A woman is swinging beside him

Truck lines zigzag up a pass
through snow the color of clinkers

Two soldiers are skinning a rabbit
the jiggling nakedness
emerges out of fur
glistening tendons
a warm flush but no blood

Wind plucks the small fire
pale yellow petals
growing in crates, cane bottoms
of broken chairs

When the men let out breath
it appears like a membrane
like the after birth of a rabbit
Their trampling about
has left shadows
half erased

The second soldier steadies
a black metal pot
suspended from three thin sticks
Water babbles away to itself

Light lowers slowly
in a sky full of snow, more snow
Two ears twitch
in the grip of the first soldier
something startled afresh
as at the moment of death

The knife severs
backbone and fur
A snowflake collides with the blade
coasts sideways
grazes the open eye

DONGO

> *"Aren't you glad I followed you to the end?"*
> — Claretta Petacci to Mussolini

Someday we come
to the less than grand finale.
"The comedy is finished!"
as Pagliacci cries out
in the opera.

At the end of a long life of posturing
above all to ourselves
we stand in the rain near Dongo
by the low wall
by the villa hidden in trees
at Giulino di Mezzegra
in the rain at five o'clock
on a cold April afternoon
wondering to ourselves
by the wet stones
and the pockmarked puddles
why the bullets took so long
took so long.

And the only other miracle
is that we are not alone.
A woman who had no reason
to join us
joins us.

If we hang
tomorrow on meathooks
in the square in Milan
in the Piazzale Loreto
side by side
slab by slab
it was not nothing
to learn after blustering
about love for a lifetime
like the poet D'Annunzio
as puffed up as D'Annunzio
as faked up as D'Annunzio
love is bread
Claretta Petacci
one loaf between two.

VIII

"Crossing the Line"

(Visitor in Other Lands)

CROSSING THE LINE

Where water turns from clockwise to counterclockwise and

the vine. Pure chance, also the laws the Traveler's Tree

obeys or dies. I write, crossing the line, as the sun's rays

striping the striped deck awning make a check of time. The sea

is ruled: birds, words, migrate upon their courses. Any

unseen equator, yes, but not the least degree of latitude.

ST. ANDREW, NORTH SHORE

Gold and white tiles, brand new, from Italy,
uncased and laid out in the sun, the late afternoon sun—
fortunate parishioners, or rich, to remake their church,
but will these marry well with the old walls?

Everything must have come once; church, people,
must have been awkward, foreign, too white, or too black,
too starkly white, or too certainly gold—
intruders all, as these, to the lush valley of St. Andrew,
the unbelievable green with the church mellowed to ivory.
It is old news, now, who came willingly
and who did not. The cattle browse, and the sun
includes everything, even the mismatched and eroded hills.

Only a stranger at odds with himself would question the tiles,
find the hour unaccountably sad, or the place too serene,
asking the best road to Bridgetown
as if he hated to leave or to stay.

— *Barbados*

BATHSHEBA

The gorge was full of trees, shadows, and monkeys
who were so large, so agile, for a while
there was no believing in them, then no disbelieving,
although the guidebook said there were none in Bathsheba.

And what a mystery the noon should be alive with monkeys,
with little brown dog masks and ghostly limbs
and quiet, complaining chatter in the trees—

then, nothing in the woods but steady shadows,
and the pale patches of the glittering sea,
the cast off rocks being battered by the foam,
and the guidebook saying there were no monkeys in Bathsheba.

— Barbados

ROAD JUNCTION NORTH OF BRIDGETOWN

Faces and figures on a wall where three roads meet,
dog masks in ocher, red, gray blue, and long necked beasts,
starting far forward, as if the shadows spelled from hands had bled
on mortar. Our traveler's supplications to these crude
gods of the fearful passage and the place. Who daubs the walls?
Whose are the unlettered messages, meant to be read
out of car windows as the stranger glances, swerves,
lost, till an avenue of royal palms retrieves the wheels
that spun, jarring the heart, here at the doubtful ground?

— Barbados

ST. LEONARD'S CHURCHYARD, BRIDGETOWN

for Anne

Who has an inkling where they'll lie for ever,
when such an accident could choose for you
this overgrown, outmoded place? Where one
of the West of England's churches, also marooned
in frangipani jungle, dates in centuries,
more than the moss on stones or English ivy
thrusts back the clock, which anyway is stopped
at what imperial hour? Add the word "London"
to the stone, as if you came from London,
not somewhere years ago, and going somewhere

Earth has to be bargained for where no provision
is made for accidents, and the Bajan parson
speaks the old burial service with a deep affection
as if he loved and buried words, and by mistake
buries you for a man under the wreaths, the radiant flowers.

Excuse all accidents for a simplicity—cast sandals
from the gravedigger's feet lie on another slab.
You, too, have lost your shoes. The Union Jack,
discreetly small, flaps on the High Commissioner's car,
discreetly small—white clouds, schoolchildren,
cutting the block to take the churchyard home …

Caught on a journey, anyway, how can this lovely,
random, unlikely place ever offend you?

— *Barbados*

211

ROSE HALL

The ancient lady in the empty house recalls
Memories more savage than romantic candlelight can soften;
And yet it softens something all the same,
As the soft water and soft-bellied moths that stitch by stitch
Take out the pattern, permanent as flame.

She sits. She fondles silver. And the rain
Brings dark runs under doors. The wind
Spreads random ghosts out of the muslin. One green stain
Is scorched above a lamp—hissing perhaps, it steams ...

If it caught fire, this house, tonight, and she were burned
(She is a little deaf and drunk as well, she would not hear
Until, herself alight, it would be far too late
To run into the storm-soaked garden and escape) ...

If she were burned,
And rent this mouldering fabric with her screams—
That no one hears—
Will this propitiate those ghosts? Will this bring peace,
At least of the cold, dampening ash, the hiding vine—
Into an old, long haunted head?

Or will this too increase,
Vaguer, these images that will not quit her shrine?

                                        — *Jamaica*

OLIVE TREES

for R.K.

"I never knew of a man,
Who'd heard of a man,
Who knew of the death
Of an olive tree,"
Said an old peasant,
Dying, to his son,
Leaving him
Acres of olive trees,
Shimmering silver green
On the slopes
Of a nearby hill.

STORM OVER LAKE COMO

First it was the frogs, belching
low Latin in the pocked slime
around stove-in boats. Then thunder
came out of the peaks and lightning
rattled the bones of the villages
scattered over the slopes. No rain.
And a strange distance to everything
as if nothing were serious—nothing
to unsettle the chandeliers in the
windows of the baroque palace or the
awnings. Only a rumor out of
the dank canal. The lovers went on
wrestling in parked cars. The heroic
dead of Trieste stayed dead in their
defendable monument. And the waiters
never troubled themselves to take in
white tablecloths, the silverware
the peaked scarlet table napkins or
the trolly with whole domed cities
of white icing and chocolate tiles.

BERGAMO

Be kind to her, police persons
(both singularly attractive).
The fact that she was riding
her motorcycle at full speed
down the Via Collioni at a danger
to everyone means only she had
somewhere to go in a hurry.
The heart has its reasons
its errands. She is so
lovely, so tearfully anxious
and you have delayed her.
Give her the smallest fine
or hurry her on with your horns
clearing the street in the hope
that whatever awaited her, waits.

IN THE PRAGUE BOTANICAL GARDENS

May 1988
for Margaret

About the Embassy each tree
is bugged, and perhaps even here
he listens, though I doubt it,
critic of our endearments, enemy
to all exaggeration. Here where
we're screened by iris, a wall
of bluer air, everything else
has fallen in neglect, reverted,
mingled: flowers, plants, perhaps
emotions. Thrown back into an Eden
before the Dutch had ordered it,
English or Chinese gardeners made
elaborate games of freedom
and illusion, we wander where no shade
interrogates its double in the shade.

Outside is Prague, packed squares
of strawgold churches, palaces,
but here the seacoast of Bohemia
shines greener after storm, tidewrack
of weeds, flotsam, jetsam, each root
a serpent. It is a paradise of spies
and yet abandoned to our hide and seek
with centuries, wondering which one's
least fun to be alive in. Love, let us
be true, if not by edict always to each
other, then to what it is, in you,
in me, joins us in joy, equivocal,
ephemeral as maybe. Let's play back
jargon, cant to birdsong, under alien
trees honor all anarchy of heart.

Here plants need no permission;
they go wild in ways too singular
to strain for definition, climb one
another like figures in some Indian
stupa. Here, tatting a leaf to lace,
a bug is just a bug; it may devour,
but not record its minutes or the
garden's. Where there's no budget
for the botanist, insect and plant
go free of history to compost,
their name unnamed in Latin, Czech,
as secretive, maybe, as secret lovers …
not lovers' secrets: Milena to Franz,
Franz to Milena in print, kept letters
under the spotted leaves of laurel.

These tubers rot in pots behind
the broken windows, a line of sheds,
gray greenhouses, unsalvageable places,
or corners where the sun writhes
in a gourd, pale, crinkled trumpets.
Here the garden ends, a boundary of
sorts, green curtain into concrete.
And here we turn. Tell me, my darling,
before we reach the gate again, enter
the city with its listeners, just
what it was we saved to say here.

LABORER NEAR BALLINROBE

His peatspade scrapes
on gravel and rabbit bones

the small teeth of the scar
his shadow makes
still darker.

His body steams already
in a coat
as red as rust or rubble,
its texture like the turf
he lifts and breaks
between his fingers —

a cool, fine fall of dirt
dropping like rain
among the harebells.

LETTER FROM ST. ANTONIN NOBLE VAL

Now that the leaves of the chestnut trees are lit
from below by the glow of the green river
winding through yellow bluffs and the easy arches
distinctly different, like asymmetrical eyebrows
loved and recalled in a clear dawn among pillows;
and now that the dogs, alert, tails twitching,
wander the pink squares of tables and butt
each guest's hand in turn for bread and the bones
of the rabbit, whose flesh came away in rosy flakes
like salmon and sweet in the dark gravy, I scatter
wine for whatever gods of the place persist, for
light that crosses the Aveyron—for luck denied,
and for you, nearer, more dear, for the distance.

NSANGWINI CAVE PAINTINGS

In the panic hour we turn and run
from the healing eland. Blood flows
from our nostrils. The trance takes hold
but the imagined wings do not
bear us up. We overlap one
another, beast / man. Legs tangle
ankle / hock. We no longer run
on own feet when we follow
in one frieze like running fire
the white veins, rock rivers. We are
no longer in our time. We are all of us
running down, running down.

— *Swaziland*

THORN: MLAWULA

We belong to our possessions
in a bitter place: red dust, stone
and the backward thorn
of the wait-a-bit bush.

Our cameras capture us like that
snag us only when moving away.
While there is light
we think of ourselves as free
lacking the bound of the impala
motionless a split-second in air—
catches in the breath
at elegance beyond our power
to bring down, use, devour.
Game escapes our game.

All we hold onto holds
even folksongs sung by the bushfire—
harmony, melody
built round the crackling of wood.
Far off, an intrusive shunting
of trains. The black ridges
of the sky, acacia, barring
the stars. I walk into night
on a leash, a chain of words, a list
of everything in the world but the world.

— *Swaziland*

Y'IEBO

"Y'iebo!"—said everywhere, but spelt ... ?
meaning "I see you!" Called out in birdlike
voices by the girls washing in rockpools
for the Reed Dance. I see you, too,
naked and waving unselfconsciously.
It is a flesh-flowered morning and I see you
against the sun splash in the water
near luminous rocks. How reassuring, where
each child who passes, every grinning stranger
calls out "I see you!" White turns to red
under the sun, or to burnt orange like the roads
of Africa, but no identity-collapse this morning.
I see you and in Swaziland, foreigner, man, "Y'iebo!"

MOZAMBIQUE

At sixteen I lost
what little virginity remained
from loving myself
to the hotel whore
of the Hotel Polana

She was fourteen
I didn't know
when she whispered
"lento mais lento"
the police chiefs
the casino owners
owned her

I have never paid
for a woman—
slow, go slowly—

When the raucous birds
retched in the dawn light
when the gardener
hunted snakes with a hoe
through the bourgainvillea
I awoke alone

I have never stopped
paying for a woman
Dogs asleep in the streets
of Lourenço Marques
cheap sunsets
sharknets and a sea
which arrived exhausted
smelling of skin

Each day on the beach
boys the color of tea
kicked a tiny black ball
with their heels—
so agile. So somber
the hallways at night

In my closet the coathangers
jangle together
like small bells
like a secret marina

DOUBLES: MALOLOTJA

At sunset
the bushfire behind
and the last blaze of mountains before
something moves from me
among upright stones.

My shadow walking on other hills
an hour after sunrise
and the blesbok browsing
each animal making two
a black figure slanted
over brown softer
than the blesbok's flanks.

But I am part gnomon, no man
a second self walking
on hills where
I do not walk, where
something of me, intruder
does not browse, does not
in this dark double
belong here, nor will.

— *Swaziland*

IX

Anarchy and Faith

IN THE IMPERIAL BALLROOM

"Marat, we're poor, and the poor stay poor."

Trained Marxists would misunderstand
the chindits barking at the gates
Their stone palaver circulates
like ice in drinks

The house detective at the Northern door
thinks "I am bored" and cleans his nails
his mind divided between glittering breast
and neat behind
under stretched satin
swinging like the lights
tango of Waterford   The rest
is lost in blur
Maracas of St Jacques
The bird of Mirabeau   Macaw

Rolls and Mercedes   Window rolled up
each dark outrider inside dry
The eye behind starred sepia glass
fixed as a basilisk's
misses the point. His own
is turned to stone
when over ha-ha moat
float flowered creepers
No jacquerie   Marat
but Jack and Jill dolled up

At midnight Cinderella's shoe
peeps by the trellis on the gazebo
No other clue
The transformation scene
is secret   sure but slow
Blue Boy at least is lost
to each collecting aunt
Berger and Bergeress
across rococo clocks
still chatter their distress
Ding Dong   Danton
No tumbrils pass   Perdu

Near dawn   the milkmaid queen
preens at a glass alone
will never pose in mobcap for David
The lover of her lap   her Jack
alarmed by no foxtrot
in clocked silk stockings
tiptoes down the hall
The Yale locks turn
jimmy in velveteen   He chooses   then withdraws
new captain of the crew
Robespierre of diamonds
greener than chartreuse   sweeter than grenadine

The house detective loses place and pay
More than a name   the proletariate lose two
The uninvited bear away
pasteboard and paste
valse triste of stones
a dragon store
of like occasions
drawn from the once imperial
now pared   now bleeding paw

ALLEY OF THE MOON

A dream

Each night I go
to meet assassins in the lane
honing their cheap blades
in a chink of stone

Where "Be Prepared"'s our motto
sotto voce, in an undertone
with Nick the ready wit we tell
the Achilles heel
of every minor Quisling
new Czar in the old

The fateful star
fuses on grinning bottles
garlic taints the air
around us as we talk
the lesser drugs
junkie the poor-Jack bodies
bare to the waist to show
the scars of sabers
ancient torturers'
aftermarks

A history of skin
spinning the broken bottle
who's out, who's in
and how the sirens
tore us from our beds
to plot another turn
for better or for worse

Our flesh
against their armor
Dum-dums in every palace dream
we curdle with a curse
the State's cold milk

Pig's Eye, Karl, Nick, Benny, and John
tonight and every night
having some time, we test
the status quo of stones
our old mad absolutes
ourselves against the rest

CHEZ RAT

"I am an anarchist, enemy to all governments," he says,
presenting his card, which says all that and gives, instead
of his degrees, his prisons and one concentration camp.
Hero, one who lives under bridges, stinks, gives up a meal
to have his calling cards white, clean, well printed.

We buy him wine, talk for an hour. But he's a bore. He has
no more to say than "I am an anarchist, enemy to all governments."
And when he goes we laugh. Not one of us will remember
the conversation after that, who print no cards, who carry
no clear line of our own into cafés, our countries' prisons.

THE JUGGLER

These giant weights, two globes of black and gold,
Press on my hands and will not take the air:
Once from my limbs I felt them rise and fall
And heard the gasp go round the village square.

Then at my feet I'd hear their coppers ring.
The beer was good. I knew what line to play—
But now I stand the spectre of this place
And hold these things I cannot throw away.

The people gape ... But how can I look down?
The seasons come, the wind drives home the rain
That chills my bone, the sun that makes me sweat,
The snow crowns me a dunce that numbs my brain.

My eyes are black, my tongue an iron spout.
In fixed grimace I lock twin rows of teeth.
The crowds are near ... I breathe like bellows still;
But am not heard. The traffic roars beneath.

My feet are stone, my limbs are like a tower.
If I could scream, or fall, or, blundering, set
These giant spheres in space all on their own
What rest I'd have! But I'm a juggler yet!

What is the world? The sparrows perch and sing ...
What was the beer I drank? The times I had?
Like nets my arms are criss-crossed now and groan
Under these balls. Their weight has made me mad.

THE LEVELLER

The King shall be my working hand
And drink with me good ale
      When King and Crown
      They tumble down
And joy shall rule the land.

Then I shall sleep in Parliament
And eat where I've a mind
Sometimes upon good English beef
Or else of foreign kind—
For we shall have good nourishment
When joy shall rule the land.

We shall not wear a suit of gray
But plumes and satin fine
And all the girls shall dress so gay
But none so pert as mine—
Oh we shall have good times I'm sure.
When joy shall rule the land.

One morning then when I awake
And find it come to hand
      The bells will ring
      And madmen sing
And crippled men shall stand
      Then praise to God
      And Parliament!
When joy shall rule the land!

OXFORD STREET

Although by day, by day
The rain
Washes the soot from these streaked walls
But never fades
The marks of weakness
And of pain
From these set faces of our friends;

And though the crowds conspire—
Oh hear at times
The small song of the heart
Out of this hardness
Through the city's side
(It is not pride
That makes you stand apart;
It is not courage
That you need to learn.)

Time will not break
To hear you sigh,
Nor give your words
More notice than the roar
Of traffic, if you come to cry—
I LOVE!—in markets
Where men sell and buy …

These are the times of daylight
In our city,
That sets the cracks in pavements out,
The lines in faces …
Where these streets lead,
Where this great crowd is thronging—
Know this, my dear,
The hundred years behind
Have left us weak
But with a finer longing.

ANNE FRANK

... That these flowers break
the pavements and the prisons;
That these words sing
after all anger dies;
That while we watch,
searching the skies for visions,
the time of some quiet element arrives ...

Ages have passed—the unexpected
Is not our guest; we are not yet aware
When all our lives are changed
And unsuspected
What is beginning moves already there.

The streets are locked,
The rain falls on the city,
And men and women cry
For bread and light
And love stronger
Than lust or pity
To guard their secret splendor
From the night—

Death takes it all
And fear of death
And living
By a slow death
To all of this they guard,
Until they shrink
Into their own fear, giving
Out of themselves
What is too rare and hard.

Tonight we celebrate no secret
But what is closed in death
And breathes and sings
And that we turn our lives to flowing
Upon the closed flower
And the broken wings.

DEFEAT

The kings come down. It's all too easy
To give up powers that never lived ...
I see a girl who lives by logic,
I know a boy who lives by rule:
The logic is things find their level,
The rule is that the strong succeed.

The kings come down. The beggars quarrel
Over the spoil and waste the land.

Kings abdicate but are not free
To wander through the streets in rags.
I know your face, no mask will do.
We talk and take the Underground.
The moral is we live, we live,
And far too much to play a part—
       A pack of liars in your pay!
       Too many daggers in your heart!

I learn by lessons no one told,
Beneath the clock I stand and stare,
And I ignore what things are not,
And I pretend what is not there:
They say you are and I agree,
While all the time I know you know
Just who you are that meets in me.
We talk—our talk is not of that;
Our signs are signs: we make no call
Upon the other, but, in fact,
What is, is, IS ... and that is all
That matters. And by lies we part.

We live—I did not say by this.
We fall—but do not mar the rule,
Success in detail and ornate,
(I have the lip-trade of the school).
These cities are of brick, no less.
To think them into dust would not
Serve other ends. I walk the ground.
My time is time. My love is love.
As good as living is my life.

Much more I hide, but, hiding, keep
That much intact. It is not life
That living kills. Life rounds it all:
The rule, the logic, and the fall;
But into death the kings go down,
Nor abdicate to keep their crown.

THOMAS

Then, when I saw their faces, I was afraid.
Yesterday so divided; and today,
United in that desperate cry—
"He lives!" ... I turned away,
Looked down the flowered hillside
To where the field of Acaldama lay
Covered in white, wild lillies;
Then watched two lizards play
About a sunspot at my feet ...
They were all ripe for madness;
Now, today, they have seen visions.
Tomorrow who can say what rumors will begin?

No. I would see Him with those wounds
That bleed no more. Once I was led astray
By all magicians, who to display their skill,
Changed into snakes and stones.
I know the signs of madness in men's eyes.

Christ, come to Thomas
In this clear light
Of ordinary day.
Then of them all
I'll give the most away.

COUNTRY PRIEST

"Thy Kingdom Come", he prays—and hopes the morrow
Will bring the same rain on the sea,
The same March wind; bread and brown eggs
And milk; the same assuring pain that throbs
Like a low fire in all his limbs; the same
Smell of damp serge, onions, and wood;
The same speech with no gift of tongues ...
World Without End—The Power and Glory
And rolling rhetoric of that ancient story.

IN MY FATHER'S HOUSE

It is not blasphemy, I hope, to pray
for taste in heaven to win the doubter in
my father. To ask that he be made familiar
with what he knew and changed, the hanging
of a picture. Is it too much to ask that nothing
jar him? Though he was open to a certain point
a robin on a Christmas card would hurt him.

I see his room with Nicholsons and Hepworths,
Moore's Underground in War and Kit Wood's harbors,
West Indian maps, perhaps, and flowers, so many
flowers. Though he responded to ideas until he died,
I beg you, let him in slowly. A liberal Englishman
who loved America, loved above all the company of
women, gave children what they asked, wrangled
with sceptics, loathed prejudice and had
illogical dislikes, and was at times ashamed of them.
He was not always right—but you would know that.

Yet taste, his own, was sacrosanct, and, unlike most,
he earned it, his very own, held in his hands like a small
boy the bird's nest and the eggs, a tender thief,
perhaps. I would not see him wounded. He let us grow
through each carbolic phase. We were disloyal and
we laughed at him, three "monster" sons with all his
tones and gestures. If he hurt others I would ask
forgiveness. And in his room a map of Cornwall, flowers.

SIMPLE DIRECTIONS

Where the roads led and vanished
at curlew shrill, wind quickened marshes
at the end of a rainy day.

Between brothers
who fought over objects once
and borrowed everything else
from each other on life leases;
who sneer at ourselves reflected
and grow fonder.

Not, now, needing to call up
the unlikely, partly shared past
to answer such questions
as where we will be this time
next year. Who never, that I remember,
walked in step on any street
or over cliffpaths where
jackdaws in angry knots
rolled over breaking sea.

I have not given up
my five years' distance ahead
of you, nor you the right
to curse me behind my back
in the voice of a ten-year-old.

We will need everything,
all the quotations from children's books
and the rest to weather the weather,
you walking badly and me boasting
knowledge of ground I never covered,
both of us photographing
one another in our head,
not to lose any light, any occasion.

ANCIENT PIETY

He bore the character of a good husband,
a good father, and a good master.

The sacks of spiders sag, a later scrawl
Cuts name and town and date into the wall.
He sleeps in cheaper stone than alabaster,
This husband, father, and kind master.

However much abused was every claim,
Time chose not to debate about his fame:
His wife is silent and his servants keep
Their gossip still beyond some green-baized sweep.

More than Memento Mori starts our fears,
Who smell the sweet musk and excreta of the mice.
The weepers, daughters. Realistic tears
Offend us in stone eyes. Bad arts suffice ...

All overdone. All easy. Shrug that weight of stone
Into the churchyard. Marrow in the bone
Aches for the earth. Old gravelore, yews,
Undone ambition, angels, prophets, news

Beyond the rattle of the clods,
Small stones that ricochet on wood and plate,
A simple name, a start, and final date.
Words in the air, then the sole mourner plods

Back to the lych gate for the bus.
"No fuss," we smile defensively: no fuss for us.
Sweetpapers, gold and crisp as leaves
Wander across the churchyard in the breeze,

Strayed from that great extravagant gold wreath
Of all our honors—ivy and oak and laurel.
Now let a wife and children quarrel
Over informal remnants of lost grief.

MARRIAGE

On that first morning he got up and went
Straight from the bed into wet meadows
Where horses grazed under the mountain
And pine trees cast their longest shadows.

He stood beside the wooden bridge and waited
And heard the creek move over rocks and poles,
He watched a blue-jay in a yellow aspen
And saw two mares come drinking with their foals.

To set a distance from that cabin door,
To watch the sun dry out the mist and dew,
To hear her call, and know his senses,
Snatched from his body, had been made anew.

MOONWORT, MONEY PLANT, OR HONESTY

There are so many names for what is broken in your head
But you will never know them. There are no lunatics
Now that the Moon is visited. Your hands play
Upon a rent doll. Something leaks out of it continually
You haven't noticed yet. No one is mad nowadays

"Mad" is for angry people. There are no enemies
Admitted past the desk. There are no dancers
Only the hushed gentility, attendants, and a dream
Of Wilis in *Giselle*. There are no names for us
Now your white room is visited, but "visitors"

There are no flowers, except the wan discs in a bowl
If something pulls for us to live leaves of the trees
Beyond the glass, the lying part of walls
After so many moons nothing disturbs your calm
Your doll's too limp to hold. You smile. We are the ravers

THREE NURSERY RHYMES

I: Song of the Mothers and Mary

Mary, Mary, what shall the Mothers say?
They have left your child,
Ours they have snatched away.
Was it in time of winter
That cruel Herod spoke?
What then said Heaven
That you alone awoke?
Mary, gentle Mary, why do you rise and go?
They have borne your child into Egypt:
But Bethlehem's children—No.

II: I know a Man ...

I know a man who's able
To profit with a gun;
He shot a rabbit through the head
And said: "What have I done!"
His wife she gave a party
And cried: "We've meat today!"
But he went slowly up the stairs
And put his gun away.
Then he went walking through the woods
And met the rabbit there
And said: "I'm very sorry".
But the rabbit only stared.

III: One Day

So you settle up and yield
Fair Grisilde in her prime,
And the plain or spotted field
Tilts into another time,
And the strange, uncertain words
Find no uses now nor will,
And the lions and the birds
Go over the last gray hill.

CATALAN

Today, under police posters
the rain has cancelled
two shiny yellow claws
stretch up from the grill
as though chickens were trapped
in the gutters

This is the end of the village
An unpaved road winds away
to a ruined mill

The two mechanics
and four laborers
backed to the wall
one August night
in a glare of headlights
were there only to make up
a number
in somebody's head

One raised his fist
one blocked his ears
He would stare down the light
He would be deaf to his death

—Man is the only animal
who guards his dead
said Miguel de Unamuno
a philosopher who had
forgotten elephants
and perhaps much else

In the kingdom of flesh and bone
of men and animals
the mistake of those
with a tragic sense
is to overlook life

Today in August
a few women go
up the road to the mill

Their heels are slanted inwards
they walk unsteadily
leaning on one another
Their dresses are lacquered
as if with the ink
of forty five years

One carries a bunch
of blue flowers
with a name in Catalan

The flowers heads are heavy
they sway, full of shadows
Gravely, they bow to the street
then, like women talking
draw closer together

MESSENGER FROM FEZ

The messenger nobody saw
pushed three shankbones over the wall
with rolled paper for marrow

names of dead friends
can wait until sundown

now in a corner of the garden
the cock pigeon
treads them like his hens
holding down each in turn
with clamps of pink wire

JEWISH FESTIVAL

for Miron Grindea

Now to the summer park
Welcome! Welcome Susanna!
The insect swarms intone
Gold syllabled hosannahs.

Aza and Azael
Stare from the gopher trees
And from Arabian cells
Journeys the queen of bees.

Your white feet on the lawn
Awake archaic kings,
The wasps and hornets clap
Their dry, seraphic wings.

The cymbals of the sun
Clash on the river's face,
Water with flute and drum
Glides into your embrace.

The elders stamp and sing,
Crickets consumed in fires,
And black rabbinic bats
Hum in the air like wires.

Jahve and Satan dance
The peace of Rosh Ha-shanah:
Now to the summer park
Welcome! Welcome Susanna!

ET INCARNATUS EST

Lord of the land made man,
Flesh of these fields,
Taking the crown of thorn,
Sceptre of reeds,
Sleep in this maiden's sleep
This night that perfect will
All earth's and heaven's needs
Rest in her still.

Time may not take her word,
Spoken once so—
Angel or shadow wait,
Watching alone,
What comes will come in time
Neither to force nor fear
She who has made her own
All that is here.

Nothing of earth nor air
That 'Yes' denies—
Bridge of our death becomes
What arc above?
Mary shall know him man
God who has chosen how
They that have borne in love
All until now.

LAZARUS

There were two walking, walking together—
I was the one, and the other also;
a dark one lingering, a light one hastening:
the dark clung to light, and the light sought shadow.

Come—said the one.
But I was neither.
Stay—said the other.
But I was neither.
The light one led me, growing darker.
The dark one lingered, a figure of light.
Still I followed. The one grew greater.
The other shrank to a child and cried:
and I felt no pity (for I was neither);
but one was lost,
and that one was I;
and I turned to go;
but I could not hold him.

Come—said the dark one—
the other is with me.
And I came with the One,
Who was only One;
and that One was I ...
and the way lay open.

      —COME—cried a voice.
And the One was two;
and I was neither.
We must go—said the one.
Stay, stay—cried the other.
And I was the one, and the other also.

      —COME—cried the Voice.
And the dark one shrank to a child of light and cried;
but I felt no pity (for I was neither);
but one was lost,
and that one was I;
and I turned to go;
but I could not hold him.

Come—said the dark one—
the other is with me.
And the two were walking, walking together;
a light one lingering, a dark one hastening:
the light clung to dark; and the dark sought daylight—
And I was the one, and the other also.

MYSTIC

for Angelus Silesius

Resting upon hands his heavy head he sees
The veins become a flowering tree
And blossom burns his eyes—
Old eyes, no longer trustworthy ...

Words all have haloes,
Music is silence perfected,
Birds have become the messengers of God
And carry blessings back and forth
Between these two old men
Out in their gardens under flowering trees.

DOVE

for Simone Weil

PRAISE: Sharp
white
and
envy
of the night—
the dove

Peace—
not of words
nor wishes
who
our wrongly reasoned longing
always eludes

Vision
immaculate

Gift
not of seeking
but of perfect love

PRAYER: Bird
and
the
Word
of
God
descend
unto
the
waiting
heart.

THE DUST OF AVILA

"We are not angels and we have bodies"
—so Teresa of Avila
who was not the right saint
for Bernini to resurrect
nor would she walk through doors
when doors could be opened
a fat fond woman
with "ridiculous" always on her lips

The body of a middle aged nun
may float in the air
like a black balloon
for a while
but it is soon down

astir in kitchens
on the highways
on behalf of friends
in the councils
where they talk of "heretics"

dust on her feet
a clove tucked into her cheek
"Save your astonishment for God"
"Find me cheap corn for my nuns"
"Save my geese from the angels"

CHAMELEON

That it changes color is not so important,
after all, it keeps the same form.
Animal magician, or a retort
that bubbles up of itself different dyes,
but with a limited repertoire.

Hypocrite. It has itself to protect.
It will wear horns and a tail to its dying day.
Metamorphosis ought to go further.
What it dreams of being is another matter.

I have known chameleons whose poor pretences
blended them only into a chair, a table—
they were found out and maimed.
Even the neutral colors of rocks
were not sufficient to hide them.

What the chameleon lacks is another shadow,
a ventriloquist's voice, or a taboo on killing chameleons.
They cannot be quite true to themselves or save themselves.
Better trust luck, I'd say, than counterfeit chameleons.

SANS

Sans arms, sans legs,
Sans belly, head—
Better to hear
The birds from bed.

Colossus' members
Scattered so,
A masterpiece
Of patient woe.

Sans power, sans voice—
His cry of need
All the king's horses
Would not heed.

Beak finds the worm
Below the ground;
A pull, a plop,
An eating sound.

Sans sex, sans eyes,
Sans entrails, sans
Oh anything—
Supinely sans.

LETTERS TO DEMETRIUS

I

Nothing the wind suggests is quite the same as names, Demetrius.
I speak as simply as I can, but the word "jadedness" enters with bread.
Today, even the songs of birds, their little disturbances, are a frenzy
I shy from. The ravages of those I love and their ravagers
are too much the history of my own head. I allow everything in in dreams.
Do not ask me if my hands are clean. I escape into eating and sleeping—
the quiet killer and rapist whose alibis are all perfect ... Well,
you are unsafely buried. I can write no one else. Another cedar
is turned upside-down over the wall it broke in its fall. Look,
the hills are filling the gap. This is Eden and we never knew it. Too bad
to be growing old without ever saying anything important except to the dead.
Some there are, the half-brave, like ancient Romans, frank only in their last wills
and what will is that? What we were given. What we give back. Oh, the
great longing to be something more than one's own bad translation, to take
the words we use and shake sense out of them at last! I accuse no one.
I was seldom there and hired substitutes. I pick up a leaf and wonder
who is it spins a leaf by its stem near the wall saying your name, Demetrius,
friend? was there ever such a thing as friendship in the world? And I, I
do not even know which Demetrius—any will do. And you in the stone,
you whose lettered name can hardly be read, talk back to the sun.

II

When the shock came, should I have invented anger? I am angry only not to
       find anger,
as if I knew what would meet from me with whatever comes from without. We
       are all
conspirators. We play games with the shadows on screens and are always the
       same
sly partners: "Think for me," "Kill for me." Sometimes I know the I who
       invents me. This is
the authentic pretence. It is less trouble to be polite to the crazy I of lies than
       go
looking for either of us, Demetrius. Even this is a form of play, of evasion. Am
       I then
in Greece, or near New Hope, Kentucky? New Hope? Is the old one then
       dead?—gone West,
all debts cancelled from Odysseusless Greece? I see it is June twenty-seventh,
the year nineteen eighty-one, in my fifty-first year ... and you?—why
       should a

Demetrius die in Kentucky? Is there comfort in this? Did you go about Melai
     to lie
in the place of storm-shaken cedars, to be stamped on in the stomping ground
     of chipmunks?
Ah, I can tell any fool that I love you, my friend, my forerunner in death,
     Demetrius.
Who knows us, who can dispute our friendship? We share secrets I will sell if I
     can.

III

Consider the loving of women with me, Demetrius. Shake the pink mallow
and trumpet the air from the trumpetvine ... This much talked-of love. Is it
     always the same?
What we say it is? What did you make of it? Or did you fake like the rest of us,
wanting of women more than anyone ever asked of us, wanting them to be
     everything
we lacked?—every one of them absolute? ... Everything we lacked, our
     authenticity above all?
No new hope but in some woman somewhere—so suicidally anxious we
     botched everything,
every encounter, every long marriage ... never content with one woman, how
     could we be?—
who wanted what was the sum of all things? Were you successful with women,
     Demetrius?
And what did you give them, despair, your poor freightload of lacking? No, the
     fables
are fables and are all around us. Simply tell me. Was there anything equal to
     women?

IV

Was the sun sufficient, Demetrius? Would you dance to be alive?—
friend, stranger? Were you, too, the half-brave? Did bread remind you
how much we have paid to be eating and daydreaming, feeding the ghost
of our will who owes everyone plenty to keep going under the trees? And who
dies out in himself all the minutes I live on asking you to join me,
you who, like Lazarus, know what it was worth at the stopping place?
Tell me, dead Demetrius, what live Demetrius never knew. Take
the quarters off your eyelids, or the obals, give me the better sense of
anger and argument. Which way to New Hope, better hope than sharing
the lies I live by and spread, all my daily dying. Get us undead, Demetrius.

X

Circe and Her Lovers

(Love and War)

CIRCE AND HER LOVERS

all in abundance the poured black of panthers almost the
bloom of damson when in sunlight the quivering fur shades
her flesh also the alert courteousness of gazelles attendant
always to her least wish as if the slightest sigh were a
disturbance in the deep sand shoals of their eyes and the
serpent mesmerized by some erotic spell of its own caressing
endlessly caressing her unsandled foot

a lizard slips over the drawn figures of her book the
great bear a white grub near its paws watches her longingly a
lion plays with her wand

the nakedness of the woman haunch buttock tail ears they play
their colors and moods touch taste scent gaze upon her
autumnal ocelot wintery badger the quick and slow seasons
of beasts few close to comatose watching with morose eyes as
unseen and enduring the brand burns others lit to the fiery
points of their pelts brush nervous by flank and knee or
dance frenzied on their four footprints before her

chameleon sorcery of color the taut fineness of her skin
almost the light green of grapes almost the same translucency
at her breasts and elsewhere olive or cornelian or rose yellow
and changing constantly changing cast shadow cast thoughts cast
memories of these who were once other than this who might still be

an owl blinking at her from his perch not caring that a mouse rubs
his silken tufts to please her under the lobe of her ear a
black goat licks her ring

THE DANAIDES

Delilah with the locks, but, Oh, ambiguous
her gaze! Does it show grief
or one more triumph of deceiving?

The camera caught her so. Was Agonistes
for Samson only—who for her Invader
was fraternizing foe, Philistia's Judith?

Within our century one Lowland Jael
despatched her German Siseras with a hatpin—
the sale boche in the bed, the open Bible.

Brought them Valhalla in a lordly bandbox.
That lepidopterous art, a hate of Hecate,
was it allowable for king and country?

Pro Patria perhaps all's fair; *horresco referens*.
She saw the foxes burning in her Flemish farmlands,
gates carried off from Ghent, the sack of Louvain.

Children cried out to her from shattered houses,
their need was bread, instead she brings them vengeance,
these lapidary scalps, this lingering folktale.

Samson's still blind, but who grinds what in Gaza?
The miller's maid with men's hair in her pillow.

ARTIST IN WARTIME

"The Duke intended to fortify the town, and so he distributed the duty of seeing to the gates among his sculptors and architects."
— Cellini

Stumbling over fire buckets in the dark hall,
He curses the blundering man. Quick round a dome
Pry the passionate fingers of light.
Bombs tumble down hundreds of stairs.

He thinks: I, once master of thought,
Made the finest distinctions in words.
Now my pamphlets make enemies weep—
They surrender, some tell me, in droves.

Resisting the Sirens when young,
I was freer than Plato. I know
Of Schoolmen deserting to trace
The scrawl of my nails on the walls.

Now it's Autumn, the sewers expound.
Yellow leaves mash in poisonous rain.
Strangers stop me: Which way to the Gate?
Is it open? I long for my room.

One door left with a key in the past.
The extinguisher's coils like a squid
Suck in darkness, the dust in the hall.
—I could tell the white flower from the snow.

Stairs grow steeper, that's age; as I climb
All the gerunds are whistling like gas.
That third name on the boarding house board—
Spy nor woman can find me: I'm OUT.

WAR

Your features, Helen—waging a ten year war
For one fair woman. Liberty.
Just claims of kings. Christ's tomb inviolate.

Your features, Helen—a hundred thousand dead
For one fair woman. A nation's pride.
Half Asia for a grazing ground.

Your features, Helen—scholars applauding murder
And for one fair woman. Mars rages innocent …
Your features, Helen.

GRAPHIC BY FRITZ PAULI

only a child walking on the waves
carrying a light
to a man with a death's head
and a skull face
on a raft
in the middle of a lake
surrounded by mountains

"Happy Christmas"
it says below
in German
and the date
"1944"

MARCH

Winter must have re-formed behind the woods.
Morning, the gathering of the lean guerillas,
old men and boys, Hunger their open password,
in ancient sheepskins nudging the black bark of trees.

Mother. A Death's Head. Shaven fields of stubble.
Hearing a rifle cocked
                              a mile away. The water
reflects the sky, reflects the water—each deepening,
each tempering the blue stain of the cold. A snowflake
lost from the host. A bird invading
through all the open, mote of the eye, dominion.

"God's punishment!" he barks. He heels the embers,
strides in his great boots, clanks with joints of steel.

A wraith, a ghost, he opens out his Bible
between the armies:
                              "One will go down in blood—the other
triumph, freeze by its guttering fires.
None will know summer." The book clumps to the earth
like a black nugget. The carcass of a crow
bumps heavy through the boughs as if to meet it.

He stands in silence, a white barn beside the water,
himself both halves, reflector and reflected.
Converging lines of men, wolves loping, woodlice
concede him his fixed point, criss-cross that landscape
on mud like rusted knives. He strikes his balance,
abandoned among flags, guns spiked, flayed peasants screaming.

FOOTNOTE TO HOMER

The horses of Zeus wept, you say
But was it for our fate or for themselves
Learning that immortality wasn't much
To boast about, whose blinders heretofore
Had kept them from the carrion on the plain?

BALLAD OF THE RAIN

Under a black thicket
In the pelting rain
She lies down
Who will not rise again.

The Moon will not watch her going,
Who passes through soil and fire—
It is a small thing to be showing,
A falling of mire to mire.

Her lips will speak no secret,
They close like the night flower;
She celebrates no difference
Upon this hour.

Woman, alone, woman—
Death by the side of the way—
Burn now in resurrection
What the rains wash away.

Angels like birds attendant
Gather what you may.
They shall find the fire gone,
        Gone also
What the rains wash away.

FOR WILFRED OWEN

Surely by this time
these barbed vines
should have borne fruit,
the pineapple grenades
sprung their foliage,
the mines
detonated poppies?

It is the oldest cliché,
we flow out into flowers,

our lives released again
in the wind and the rain
along ramparts,
our bright eyes
are plucked by children
to be crammed into jamjars,

we inhabit white bowls
in the buttery farmhouses,

we are crushed under wagon wheels
and our sap stains the lovers.

We turned our backs
upon love
and the young girls gather us.

Our wives will wear black,
and the young girls gather us.

Long before Homer our metaphor
was the reaping and springing
of flowers.

Sentimental as soldiers
once
who sang along lanes—

surely these fields should be filled
with the fragrance of flowers.

PATH UNDER THE MEDLARS

Autumn how far exceeds our expectations
overflowing the barns and still
the brown mash of windfalls
under our feet and the air
overburdened with apples

The wild fruit of abandoned trees
bringing the boughs down before
white cottage doorways. Everything breaking
and the wasps too glutted to fly

but in frenzied circles, knowing no way out
of impossible surfeit. October, November
and long after apples, the medlars
overripe in their skins and everywhere
musk of medlars. And why is this year so
generous? Why only to trees no one has tended

these hundred years? Walking dark ways
in the rain and the raindrops sweetened and
colored like sap and the smell lingering, tell me
were we too prudent? Were we? Let everything go.
Let the years go. Let love that most
overhusbanded, overwifed thing Go!

CARNIVAL IN TIME OF PLAGUE

Shadows on sleeves, the nightingale
sings in a maze of thorn, tabor
and lute have echoes like withdrawing
seas. We made our promises, sealed with
our lips, body to breathing body—O
Polio, Polio, Polio, the bee stings
deep that dies upon his sting. I wear
the rose still fresh. Shadow on every-
thing. Today I loved you and tonight alone.

To hate May music for your sake,
to take a madman's rake and smash the moon
on water, or to lie in limepits for the
company of saints? Run out that ripple to
the furthest reed. Nothing cancels the song,
nothing extends the song, nothing consoles …
if it weren't so, I was your lover only for the
love. So fleeting, so they say. Today
I lay beside you, and tonight, alone.

So fleeting, let not pettiness pretend, or
clamor shake the stillness where you sleep.
I have no tears. Whatever envy won, won and
is done. Your dying was no less than all
the ugliness I knew. After the dance, the
carrion. Let it be. It touches nothing that
has taken all. Polio, break hands. Say to
the stars I lived to dance with Polio.
There is no boast so desperate true. Say
for today, we kept our promises.

EVENING IN FERRARA

Even the Corso is quiet, and the cats
walk with the ghosts of executioners
between their angular shoulders.
Linen sellers' booths flap
in a hot wind, and the pigeons
safe from the children who clear
the Piazza of birds by day, sleep
on their roosts of dung and straw
among saints. The last Este
is duke of roots. The last bus has left
for Bologna. Peace, stars, and
astronomers. The frescoed lovers are dead,
without care, *schifanoia*, dead,
leaving lute music plucking at air.

SNAKE

It is not so much the eyes that hypnotize
but the alluring movement
the sensual contact between body and ground
or bough, or rock

all surfaces are to the snake excitement
of a sort most men only know in dreams
succubus and incubus of the earth

it is the limb that slides over the limb
cold skin passing quickening of skin
nothing else is exchanged in those seconds
but the soft hissing together of breath

IN TIME OF PLENTY

Abundance is in all things
If not the thing itself
then the dream of its fullness

AZAEL of the balances
bring me the green apple

Neutral
having the equal weight of the one
and the weight of the other

Is thirsting for water the same as drinking
or better?

This is to sharpen both sides
against the middle

and what is the middle state of love?

In her absence I dream of her presence
and in her presence I dream of her absence

There is no middle state of love
There is only *having* and *fear of losing*
and, occasionally, *fear of having*

all together in abundance

In abundance the dream and the shadow and the thing itself
Go and find and fetch and bring by the longest way possible
Tarry and stay for the longest time possible
Be
I would rather starve eating than feast upon the idea of eating

TO MARGARET ...

The hunger of the seabird in the sky—
To mimic his raw greed,
To cry his cry,
To send his great, barbed shadow
Through your eye.

EPITHALAMION

Morning for marriage in this stormy August—
Early with orioles, tanagers, and cardinals,
Gentlest of brides, the groomsmen's song
Hushed Peachtree traffic, distanced Emory bells.
Awoke you when day broke in higher trees.
Now guest by guest in white with wider welcome comes
Across long lawns of evening in the firefly light;
Neighbor by neighbor, grave and giggling throng,
Drawn to the organ's bourdon and the rap-tap drum.
Call then to quieting nest "All peace is here." Atlanta
Lights up the bridal chamber in an oriole glow.
All merriment, all "friend" to "more," all whispered love
Religion binds, one August for all time. You whisperers,
Keeping your holy cricket secrets and your present pledge.
Earth/Heaven endure in vows. The song fades on the song.

ROADS

Ten years ago, I'd not have met you
in these mountains. Lying on pebbles
you read Montale's *Eastbourne* to me.
The Kentish wind rasped in the dunegrass,
even the sound was cold for August.

The spent sea turned the shingle over
in time but not in tune, watch
on a watchchain. Days of cloudrace.
Brass bands, my Dora Markus, harvest
wife. Two weeks to walk in orchards.

Do not desert me any hour between us
whatever sadness. Cedars and shacks,
churches foursquare as tombstones
sending slant shadows through tobacco.
The tall corn in the bottoms. All ways

from Wingham's oaks and crows
upon the backroads. Red iron bridges
over rumbling planks ... Search in your
handbag. You've got the pebbles
somewhere. Your opal ring's on fire,

your hair's as red as brambles
with the setting sun. "Caw, caw."
Crows settle and away from Wingham.
Range after range to climb,
Kentucky, part of Tennessee.
Night darkens but we know the roads.

AMOUR PROPRE: CLARENCE

My shadow cuts in two
The Piazza San Marco,
I go by water
To London and Basra.
You who pass by,
Keep time with my cane;
I may never walk
Down this same street again.

In the eyes of my mistress
I see only my own,
I look quite distinguished
At this time of day.
You who pass by,
Listen for my name;
I may never repeat it
The same way again.

When I look at a portrait
The glass shows me mine
I straighten my tie
And brush my lapel.
You who pass by,
Look now in this frame;
I may never choose
The same picture again.

You who pass by,
Forget that I am vain:
Memorize my features,
I may not live again.

DON JUAN IN WINTER

Women like mirrors yet who plot with Fate,
catch my grimace, return it still a smile,
darken your luster! I have learned to hate
what no return through you can reconcile.

My snares, my plots, take ribbons from your hair;
disguised as doves my crows are powdered things;
my flattering words have all their hindparts bare;
when I croak "Morning" all the orchard sings.

You enemy to sleep, dear What's-your-name?,
summon more play and have the loser's right.
Call off the pack! You have confused the game;
though I cheat still I fumble in plain sight.

My Hearts changed Spades chime on the frozen turf;
my Diamonds clump like coal the forest floor;
red spots lead huntsmen to some reeking earth;
black suits nailed grinning on a barnyard door.

Dear, clocks cluck time, cards fall like giant flakes.
Through that cloth arch, beyond the windows, lie
the parklands gray with dawn, the winter lakes
stacked with black antlers where beasts lock and die.

VENICE

She sleeps upon her back, I think, this city;
Warm as a sleeping woman are her walls,
And there are sounds of breathing often in her alleys
At noon or night, above chance calls
Of children in some other street, the water lapping,
And boats that leave her—always leaving,
Carrying, perhaps, as great a coward as Æneas
Beyond her waking and her grieving.

BETHANY

Once, they came seeking Lazarus
Up the winding dirt road to Bethany
To learn about death. "What was it like?"—
So many tourists, so much chattering.

That was before Titus came, of course,
And made Lazarus with all the rest a prisoner
To try the steadiness of raw recruits for death,
Punching their short swords into packed flesh of prisoners.

And Lazarus was an old man then, in the first rank.
The sweating greenhorns missed him once and came again.
"What was it like?" Lazarus was asking those dumb Romans—
"What was it like? Life, I mean, life?"

GIFTS

On the first morning after we met
there arrived
a hundred Shiraz roses;
on the second
four trays of rubies.

Such abundance
emphasized, alas,
a lack of vases
and the narrowness
of my doorway.

It was not proportionate,

nor were the peacocks' feathers,
nor the jasmine bushes.

After a week
a pharos was built
against one wall of the house,
a minaret against the other,
two galleries overlooking the river ...

Such gifts
were like sherbets
for the janizary,

and how can I keep gazelles, my dear,
in such a small garden?

About the Author

Michael Mott was born in London in 1930. His mother was an American, his father English. He was educated in America and England and left England in 1966 to teach at Kenyon College. His first collection of poetry, *The Cost of Living,* was published in London in 1957. Mott has gone on to publish seven more books of poetry, two novels, two children's novels, and a best selling biography of Thomas Merton. Apart from teaching at Kenyon, where he was poetry editor of the *Kenyon Review,* Mott has been twice writer-in-residence at the College of William and Mary, and he has taught at Emory University, the State University of New York at Buffalo (Summer 1978), and Bowling Green State University (1980-92). He retired Emeritus and currently lives in Williamsburg, Virginia, with his wife, Emma Lou Powers.

About the Artist of "Ghost Shirt"

Margaret Ann Mott, born Margaret Watt, was a weaver known throughout the Southeast for her textile works – now in a number of museums and collections. Born in England, brought up in India, she married Michael in 1961. She died in 1990.

THE ANHINGA PRIZE FOR POETRY SERIES

Out of print

RECENT BOOKS
FROM ANHINGA PRESS

The Secret History of Water
Silvia Curbelo, 1997

This Once
Nick Bozanic, 1997

*Runaway with Words: A Short Course on Poetry
and How to Take It with You*
Joann Gardner, 1998

*Runaway with Words: A Collection of Poems
from Florida's Youth Shelters*
Edited and Introduced by Joann Gardner, 1997

Walking Back from Woodstock
Earl S. Braggs, 1997

Hello Stranger: Beach Poems
Robert Dana, 1996

*Isle of Flowers:
Poems by Florida's Individual Artist Fellows*
Donna J. Long, Helen Pruitt Wallace, Rick Campbell, eds., 1995

*Unspeakable Strangers:
Descents into the Dark Self, Ascent into the Light*
Van K. Brock, 1995

The Secret Life of Moles
P. V. LeForge, 1992

North of Wakulla: An Anthology
M. J. Ryals and D. Decker, eds., 1988